Name Server Operations and
DNS Configuration Using BIND

BIND 9 DNS Administration Reference Book

Mary Stahl, David Conrad, et al.

Edited by Jeremy C. Reed
Published by Reed Media Services

BIND 9 DNS Administration Reference Book:
Name Server Operations and DNS Configuration Using BIND
September 2007

By Mary Stahl, David Conrad, et al.

ISBN: 0-9790342-1-3
ISBN-13: 978-0-9790342-1-3

Publisher: Reed Media Services
Book Editor: Jeremy C. Reed

Contents

Preface

Welcome to the BIND 9 DNS Administration Reference Book covering DNS and the BIND software suite.

The Berkeley Internet Name Domain (BIND) implements a domain name server for a number of operating systems. This book provides basic information about the installation and care of the Internet Systems Consortium (ISC) BIND version 9 software package for system administrators. This book includes the definitive reference of the configuration syntax and grammar for *named* and the usage and command line switches for the BIND programs.

This version of the book corresponds to BIND version 9.5 and also covers some differences between older versions.

This book is based on documentation that is included with the BIND source code, including ISC's BIND 9 Administrator Reference Manual (originally by Mary Stahl, David Conrad, and the BIND 9 Development Team). The editor for this printed book provided hundreds of improvements to ISC which were integrated into the official documentation. The main differences between this book and the original reference manual are: reorganization of content, extra examples, new content, man pages and other documentation merged in, cross-referencing, indexing, and formatting for book use. For complete details about this book, please see the website at http://www.reedmedia.net/books/bind-dns/.

Copyrights and Licenses

The original materials and this book are open source. The following are the copyrights and licenses found in the original materials:

Acknowledgments

Thank you to ISC for providing the original manuals that this book is mostly based on.

Thank you to Mark Andrews and Rob Austein at ISC for providing valuable feedback and information for this book and also for helping with committing improvements back into the original source.

Thank you to Glen Turner of AARNet (Australia's Academic & Research Network) and Karl Hanmore of AusCERT (Computer Emergency Response Team for Australia) for feedback about the security documentation and for providing permission to reuse content from an AusCERT advisory.

Thank you to Stacey Marshall of Sun for providing feedback and documentation about differences between versions of BIND.

Thank you to Rob Smith for reviewing the book.

This book includes open source licensed documentation written by numerous authors and contributors. Acknowledgment and enormous thanks are due to: Mark Andrews, Rob Austein, James Brister, Andrew Cherenson, David Conrad, Michael Graff, Andreas Gustafsson, Bob Halley, David Hankins, Stephen Jacob, Ashley Kitto, David Lawrence, Jeremy C. Reed, Michael Sawyer, Mary Stahl, Jinmei Tatuya, Glen Turner, Brian Wellington, Chris Yarnell, and the BIND 9 development team. The complete list of contributors is unknown. (Please let us know of any other documentation contributors.) Thank you for your contributions to the ISC BIND documentation.

Typographic Conventions

In this document, the following general typographic conventions are used:

To describe a pathname, filename, program or command name, *hostname, or new term or concept, the italic style is used.*

`To describe literal user input, the fixed width bold style is used.`

`To describe program output, the fixed width style is used.`

The following conventions are used in descriptions of the BIND configuration file:

To describe keywords, the bold style is used.

`To describe variables or values, an italic fixed width style is used.`

To describe optional input, [text enclosed in square brackets] is used.

In long command line examples, a trailing backslash can be used literally to mean the following line is part of same command line. Long lines that end with ⇓ (down arrow) mean that the following line in the book should be read (or used) as being on the same line.

1. The Domain Name System (DNS)

The Internet Domain Name System (DNS) consists of the syntax to specify the names of entities in the Internet in a hierarchical manner, the rules used for delegating authority over names, and the system implementation that actually maps names to Internet addresses. DNS data is maintained in a group of distributed hierarchical databases.

The purpose of this book is to explain the installation and upkeep of the BIND (Berkeley Internet Name Domain) software package, and it begins by reviewing the fundamentals of the Domain Name System (DNS) as they relate to BIND.

1.1. DNS Fundamentals

The Domain Name System (DNS) is a hierarchical, distributed database. It stores information for mapping Internet host names to IP addresses and vice versa, mail routing information, and other data used by Internet applications.

Clients look up information in the DNS by calling a *resolver* library, which sends queries to one or more *name servers* and interprets the responses. The BIND 9 software distribution contains a name server, *named*, and two resolver libraries, *liblwres* and *libbind*.

1.2. Domains and Domain Names

The data stored in the DNS is identified by *domain names* that are organized as a tree according to organizational or administrative boundaries. Each node of the tree, called a *domain*, is given a label. The domain name of the node is the concatenation of all the labels on the path from the node to the *root* node. This is represented in written form as a string of labels listed from right to left and separated by dots. A label need only be unique within its parent domain.

For example, a domain name for a host at the company Example, Inc. could be *ourhost.example.com*, where *com* is the top level domain to which *ourhost.example.com* belongs, *example* is a subdomain of *com*, and *ourhost* is the name of the host.

For administrative purposes, the name space is partitioned into areas called *zones*, each starting at a node and extending down to the leaf nodes or to nodes where other zones start. The data for each zone is stored in a *name server*, which answers queries about the zone using the *DNS protocol*.

The data associated with each domain name is stored in the form of *resource records* (RRs). Some of the supported resource record types are described in the section 11.1.

For more detailed information about the design of the DNS and the DNS protocol, please refer to the standards documents listed in Appendix C.

1.3. Zones

To properly operate a name server, it is important to understand the difference between a *zone* and a *domain*.

As stated previously, a zone is a point of delegation in the DNS tree. A zone consists of those contiguous parts of the domain tree for which a name server has complete information and over which it has authority. It contains all domain names from a certain point downward in the domain tree except those which are delegated to other zones. A delegation point is marked by one or more *NS records* in the parent zone, which should be matched by equivalent NS records at the root of the delegated zone.

For instance, consider the *example.com* domain which includes names such as *host.aaa.example.com* and *host.bbb.example.com* even though the *example.com* zone includes only delegations for the *aaa.example.com* and *bbb.example.com* zones. A zone can map exactly to a single domain, but could also include only part of a domain, the rest of which could be delegated to other name servers. Every name in the DNS tree is a *domain*, even if it is *terminal*, that is, has no *subdomains*. Every subdomain is a domain and every domain except the root is also a subdomain. The terminology is not intuitive and it is suggested that you read RFCs 1033, 1034 and 1035 to gain a complete understanding of this difficult and subtle topic.

Though BIND is called a "domain name server", it deals primarily in terms of zones. The master and slave declarations in the named.conf file specify zones, not domains.[1] When you ask some other site if it is willing to be a slave server for your *domain*, you are actually asking for slave service for some collection of zones.

1.4. Authoritative Name Servers

Each zone is served by at least one *authoritative name server*, which contains the complete data for the zone. To make the DNS tolerant of server and network failures, most zones have two or more authoritative servers, on different networks.

Responses from authoritative servers have the "authoritative answer" (AA) bit set in the response packets. This makes them easy to identify when debugging DNS configurations using tools like *dig* (see section 6.1).

[1] The master and slave terminology is covered in the upcoming sections.

1.4.1. The Primary Master

The authoritative server where the master copy of the zone data is maintained is called the *primary master* server, or simply the *primary*. Typically it loads the zone contents from some local file edited by humans or perhaps generated mechanically from some other local file which is edited by humans. This file is called the *zone file* or *master file*.

In some cases, however, the master file may not be edited by humans at all, but may instead be the result of dynamic update operations.

1.4.2. Slave Servers

The other authoritative servers, the *slave* servers (also known as *secondary* servers) load the zone contents from another server using a replication process known as a *zone transfer*. Typically the data are transferred directly from the primary master, but it is also possible to transfer it from another slave. In other words, a slave server may itself act as a master to a subordinate slave server.

1.4.3. Stealth Servers

Usually all of the zone's authoritative servers are listed in NS records in the parent zone. These NS records constitute a *delegation* of the zone from the parent. The authoritative servers are also listed in the zone file itself, at the *top level* or *apex* of the zone. You can list servers in the zone's top-level NS records that are not in the parent's NS delegation, but you cannot list servers in the parent's delegation that are not present at the zone's top level.

A *stealth server* is a server that is authoritative for a zone but is not listed in that zone's NS records. Stealth servers can be used for keeping a local copy of a zone to speed up access to the zone's records or to make sure that the zone is available even if all the "official" servers for the zone are inaccessible.

A configuration where the primary master server itself is a stealth server is often referred to as a "hidden primary" configuration. One use for this configuration is when the primary master is behind a firewall and therefore unable to communicate directly with the outside world.

1.5. Caching Name Servers

The resolver libraries provided by most operating systems are *stub resolvers*, meaning that they are not capable of performing the full DNS resolution process by themselves by talking directly to the authoritative servers. Instead, they rely on a local name server to perform the resolution on their behalf. Such a server is called a *recursive* name server; it performs *recursive lookups* for local clients.

To improve performance, recursive servers cache the results of the lookups they perform. Since the processes of recursion and caching are intimately connected, the terms *recursive server* and *caching server* are often used synonymously.

The length of time for which a record may be retained in the cache of a caching name server is controlled by the Time To Live (TTL) field associated with each resource record.

1.5.1. Forwarding

Even a caching name server does not necessarily perform the complete recursive lookup itself. Instead, it can *forward* some or all of the queries that it cannot satisfy from its cache to another caching name server, commonly referred to as a *forwarder*.

There may be one or more forwarders, and they are queried in turn until the list is exhausted or an answer is found. Forwarders are typically used when you do not wish all the servers at a given site to interact directly with the rest of the Internet servers. A typical scenario would involve a number of internal DNS servers and an Internet firewall. Servers unable to pass packets through the firewall would forward to the server that can do it, and that server would query the Internet DNS servers on the internal server's behalf.

1.6. Name Servers in Multiple Roles

The BIND name server can simultaneously act as a master for some zones, a slave for other zones, and as a caching (recursive) server for a set of local clients.

However, since the functions of authoritative name service and caching/ recursive name service are logically separate, it is often advantageous to run them on separate server machines. A server that only provides authoritative name service (an *authoritative-only* server) can run with recursion disabled, improving reliability and security. A server that is not authoritative for any zones and only provides recursive service to local clients (a *caching-only* server) does not need to be reachable from the Internet at large and can be placed inside a firewall.

2. BIND Resource Requirements

2.1. Hardware requirements

DNS hardware requirements have traditionally been quite modest. For many installations, servers that have been pensioned off from active duty have performed admirably as DNS servers.

The DNSSEC features of BIND 9 may prove to be quite CPU intensive however, so organizations that make heavy use of these features may wish to consider larger systems for these applications. BIND 9 is fully multithreaded, allowing full utilization of multiprocessor systems for installations that need it.

2.2. CPU Requirements

CPU requirements for BIND 9 range from i486-class machines for serving of static zones without caching, to enterprise-class machines if you intend to process many dynamic updates and DNSSEC signed zones, serving many thousands of queries per second.

2.3. Memory Requirements

The memory of the server has to be large enough to fit the cache and zones loaded off disk. The **max-cache-size** option[1] can be used to limit the amount of memory used by the cache, at the expense of reducing cache hit rates and causing more DNS traffic. Additionally, if additional section caching is enabled, the **max-acache-size** option can be used to limit the amount of memory used by the mechanism.[2] It is still good practice to have enough memory to load all zone and cache data into memory – unfortunately, the best way to determine this for a given installation is to watch the name server in operation. After a few weeks the server process should reach a relatively stable size where entries are expiring from the cache as fast as they are being inserted.

[1]The cache memory limit option is described on page 118.

[2]Details about additional section caching can be found in section 10.25.

2.4. Name Server Intensive Environment Issues

For name server intensive environments, there are two alternative configurations that may be used. The first is where clients and any second-level internal name servers query a main name server, which has enough memory to build a large cache. This approach minimizes the bandwidth used by external name lookups. The second alternative is to set up second-level internal name servers to make queries independently. In this configuration, none of the individual machines needs to have as much memory or CPU power as in the first alternative, but this has the disadvantage of making many more external queries, as none of the name servers share their cached data.

3. Installation

3.1. Supported Operating Systems

ISC BIND 9 compiles and runs on a large number of Unix-like operating systems and on NT-derived versions of Microsoft Windows, such as:

- AIX 5L
- BSD/OS 4.2
- COMPAQ Tru64 UNIX 5.1B
- Debian GNU/Linux 2.2, 3.0
- DragonFly 1.7.0
- FreeBSD 4.10, 5.2.1, 6.2
- HP-UX 10.20, 11.11
- Mac OS X 10.1, 10.3.8
- Mandrake 8.1
- NetBSD 1.5, 2.x, 3.x, 4.x
- OpenBSD 2.6, 2.8, 2.9, 3.1, 3.6, 3.8
- Red Hat Linux 7.1
- Slackware Linux 7.x, 8.0, 8.1
- Solaris 8, 9, 9 (x86)
- SuSE Linux 7.0
- UnixWare 7.1.1
- Windows NT/2000/XP/2003

3.2. Build and Install from Source

BIND 9 currently requires a UNIX system with an ANSI C compiler, basic POSIX support, and a 64-bit integer type.

See the README and FAQ files included in the BIND source for details on specific platforms and known compiler and build issues.

The source code can be downloaded via the http://www.isc.org/sw/bind/ website. The mirror sites for downloads can be found at http://www.isc.org/sw/MIRRORS.html. Download the "bind9" tarball ending with the ".tar.gz" extension[1] for the desired release (such as ISC's official current release).[2]

Extract the source tarball using *tar*, such as:

```
tar xzf bind-9.x.tar.gz
```

Or:

```
pax -rzf bind-9.x.tar.gz
```

Replace the filename with correct filename of the source archive file. Then *cd* into the new directory (replace the *x* with the correct version):

```
cd bind-9.x
```

To build, just run:

```
./configure
make
```

The configure step will use the defaults and detect prerequisites on your system for the build (which is done with *make*).

Then to do the installation (to the default */usr/local/* directory), run as the superuser:

```
make install
```

The source code is about 6 MB and uses about 30 MB when extracted. The build uses approximately 104 MB. The new installation takes around 50 MB (depending on the configure options).

[1] The ".zip" files provide Windows Binary Kits.

[2] Download using *lynx, w3m, fetch, curl, wget*, or *ftp*, for example.

3.2.1. Advanced Build Steps

Do not use a parallel "make".

Several environment variables that can be set before running configure will affect compilation:

CC The C compiler to use. configure tries to figure out the right one for supported systems.

CFLAGS C compiler flags. Defaults to include -g and/or -O2 as supported by the compiler.

STD_CINCLUDES System header file directories. Can be used to specify where add-on thread or IPv6 support is, for example. Defaults to empty string.

STD_CDEFINES Any additional preprocessor symbols you want defined. Defaults to empty string.

Possible settings:

Change the default syslog facility of *named*/*lwresd*:

-DISC_FACILITY=LOG_LOCAL0

Enable DNSSEC signature chasing support in *dig*:

-DDIG_SIGCHASE=1 (sets -DDIG_SIGCHASE_TD=1 and -DDIG_SIGCHASE_BU=1)

Disable dropping queries from particular well known ports:

-DNS_CLIENT_DROPPORT=0

Disable support for "**rrset-order fixed**":

-DDNS_RDATASET_FIXED=0

LDFLAGS Linker flags. Defaults to empty string.

The following need to be set when cross compiling.

BUILD_CC The native C compiler.

BUILD_CFLAGS (optional)

BUILD_CPPFLAGS (optional)

Possible setting:

-DNEED_OPTARG=1 (optarg is not declared in <unistd.h>)

BUILD_LDFLAGS (optional)

BUILD_LIBS (optional)

To build shared libraries, specify "- -with-libtool" on the configure command line.

For the server to support DNSSEC, you need to build it with crypto support. You must have OpenSSL 0.9.5a or newer installed and specify "- -with-openssl" on the configure command line.[3] If OpenSSL is installed under a nonstandard prefix, you can tell configure where to look for it using "- -with-openssl=/prefix".

To build libbind (the BIND 8 resolver library), specify "- -enable-libbind" on the configure command line.

On some platforms, BIND 9 can be built with multithreading support, allowing it to take advantage of multiple CPUs. You can specify whether to build a multithreaded BIND 9 by specifying "- -enable-threads" or "- -disable-threads" on the configure command line. The default is operating system dependent.

If your operating system has integrated support for IPv6, it will be used automatically. If you have installed KAME IPv6 separately, use "- -with-kame[=*PATH*]" to specify its location.

"**`make install`**" will install *named* and the various BIND 9 libraries. By default, installation is into */usr/local*, but this can be changed with the "- -prefix" option when running "configure".

You may specify the option "- -sysconfdir" to set the directory where configuration files like "named.conf" go by default, and "- -localstatedir" to set the default parent directory of "run/named.pid". For backwards compatibility with BIND 8, - -sysconfdir defaults to */etc* and - -localstatedir defaults to */var* if no - -prefix option is given. If there is a - -prefix option, sysconfdir defaults to "$prefix/etc" and localstatedir defaults to "$prefix/var".

To see additional configure options, run "**`configure --help`**". Note that the help message does not reflect the BIND 8 compatibility defaults for sysconfdir and localstatedir.

If you're planning on making changes to the BIND 9 source, you should also "**`make depend`**". If you're using Emacs, you might find "**`make tags`**" helpful.

If you need to re-run configure please run "**`make distclean`**" first. This will ensure that all the option changes take.

Building with gcc is not supported, unless gcc is the vendor's usual compiler (e.g. the various BSD systems and Linux).

A limited test suite can be run with "**`make test`**". Many of the tests require you to configure a set of virtual IP addresses on your system, and some require Perl; see bin/tests/system/README for details.

Provide XML Stats via HTTP

The *named* server can be built to provide statistics in XML format. This is documented with the **stats-server** option on page 99.

[3]At the time this book went to press, ISC recommended using OpenSSL version 0.9.8d/0.9.7l or newer.

To build *named* with this support, use the configure switch: "--with-libxml2". It needs libxml 2.6.x or newer installed. It is usually pre-installed or easily available for many Unix systems. The homepage for libxml2 is at http://xmlsoft.org/. If the libxml2 installation is not in a standard location, use "**`./configure --with-libxml2=PATH`**", where *PATH* contains the *bin/xml2-config* tool.

3.3. Installation using Pre-built Packages

Many vendors and distributions include ready-to-use packages for their operating systems.

Note that the provide packages may have different version numbers than the official ISC packages. Nevertheless, the package vendor may have added bug fixes or improvements.

3.3.1. Installation using RPMs on Red Hat Linux

Red Hat Linux, CentOS, Fedora, and similar systems provide RPMs for BIND components. Example RPM packages are:

bind-libs Contains libraries (such as libdns, libisc, libisccc, libisccfg, and liblwres) as used by both the bind server package as well as the utilities packages.

bind This package includes *named*, *lwresd*, *rndc*, and various supplementary BIND configuration tools. It also provides documentation and configurations, such as */etc/rc.d/init.d/named* and */etc/logrotate.d/named.*

bind-utils Contains the Dynamic DNS update utility and DNS query tools *dig*, *host*, and *nslookup.*

caching-nameserver Provides simple, ready-to-use configurations (including */etc/named.conf* and local zones) for a a simple caching nameserver.

bind-chroot This package contains a directory tree and sets up a chroot jail for *named* by moving files, and creating symlinks and needed devices.

system-config-bind or redhat-config-bind Provides a graphical interface for configuring BIND. Some consider this useful for new users or for systems with small zone(s). This

bind-devel Includes files and libraries needed for BIND DNS development. It includes: archive libraries (not shared), headers, documentation with 26 IETF drafts and 89 RFCs, and developer manpages for lightweight resolver functions. This package is not needed for normal BIND usage.

On a system using YUM for package installations, you can install the several packages with:

```
yum install bind bind-chroot bind-libs bind-utils
```

To enable it at boot time on a Red Hat system, do:

```
chkconfig named on
```

It can be started with:

```
/sbin/service named reload
```

Or:

```
/etc/init.d/named start
```

3.3.2. Installation on Debian or Ubuntu Linux

Debian Linux also (like Red Hat) split up BIND into multiple packages:

bind9 Provides the *named* server and related configuration files, such as */etc/bind/named.conf* and */etc/init.d/bind9*.

bind9-host Provides the *host* utility.

libdns Shared library used by BIND's daemons and clients. (Package may include library version as part of name, such as libdns5, libdns16, or libdns21.)

libbind Provides shared library. (Package may be named like libbind9-0.)

libisc Provides shared library. (Package may be named libisc4, libisc7, or libisc11 for example.)

libisccfg Provides shared library for daemons and clients to read and write configuration files. (Package may be named like libisccfg0 or libisccfg1.)

libbind-dev This package provides static (archive) libraries and include headers for developers or to compile other software needing the DNS functions. (This package is not needed for normal BIND administration.)

libisccc Provides the command channel shared library. (Package may include library version in package name, like libisccc0.)

liblwres Shared library for the lightweight resolver library. (Package may be named like liblwres1 or liblwres9.)

lwresd Provides the lightweight resolver daemon.

dnsutils Provides various BIND client utilities.

bind9-doc Contains various documentation files.

BIND can be installed on a Debian-type system with:

```
apt-get install bind9 bind9-doc dnsutils
```

And the *named* server can be started with:

```
/etc/init.d/bind9 start
```

3.4. Locations of Files

The BIND suite provides many tools and hundreds of files. This book may mention file locations that are different than the installation or hard-coded defaults of BIND on your system.

A default build of BIND will install the server at */usr/local/sbin/named* which will use the default */etc/named.conf* configuration.[4]

Other systems may have the software at */usr/sbin/named* and the main configuration at */etc/bind/named.conf*, */usr/local/etc/named.conf*, */etc/namedb/named.conf*, */var/named/etc/named.conf*, */var/named/chroot/etc/named.conf*, or other location. This also applies to the default locations for *rndc.conf* and *rndc.key*.

Be sure to carefully check your system to see where your tools and configurations are located. Also check for a **directory** option in your *named.conf* file.[5]

[4]BIND doesn't install a default *named.conf* configuration.

[5]See page 98 for details about the **directory** option.

4. Name Server Operations

This chapter describes the *named* server and the *rndc* tool for controlling and debugging the name server daemon.

4.1. named

The *named* program is the BIND server.

When invoked without arguments, *named* will read the default configuration file *named.conf* (as covered in chapter 9), read any initial data, and listen for queries.

```
named [-4] [-6] [-c config-file] [-d debug-level] [-f]
  [-g] [-m flag] [-n #cpus] [-p port] [-s] [-t directory]
  [-u user] [-v] [-x cache-file]
```

4.1.1. named Options

-4

Use IPv4 only even if the host machine is capable of IPv6. -4 and -6 are mutually exclusive.

-6

Use IPv6 only even if the host machine is capable of IPv4. -4 and -6 are mutually exclusive.

-c *config-file*

Use *config-file* as the configuration file instead of the default, */etc/named.conf*.[1] To ensure that reloading the configuration file continues to work after the server has changed its working directory due to to a possible directory option in the configuration file, *config-file* should be an absolute pathname.

-d *debug-level* Set the daemon's debug level to *debug-level*. Debugging traces from *named* become more verbose as the debug level increases.

-f

Run the server in the foreground (i.e. do not daemonize).

[1] See section 3.4 about locations of the configuration file.

-g

Run the server in the foreground and force all logging to stderr.

-i *pid-file*

This switch is used by *named* when ran as *lwresd*. Use the *pid-file* as the PID file instead of the default, */var/run/lwresd.pid*. This is not used for the *named* name server. See section 8.2.

-l

Run *named* as the lightweight resolver daemon, *lwresd*, only. See section 8.2.

-m *flags*

Turn on memory usage debugging flags. Possible *flags* are usage, trace, record, size, and mctx. These correspond to the ISC_MEM_DEBUGXXXX flags described in <isc/mem.h>.

-n *#cpus*

Create *#cpus* worker threads to take advantage of multiple CPUs. If not specified, *named* will try to determine the number of CPUs present and create one thread per CPU. If it is unable to determine the number of CPUs, a single worker thread will be created.

-p *port*

Listen for queries on port *port*. If not specified, the default is port 53.

-s

Write memory usage statistics to stdout on exit.

Note: This option is mainly of interest to BIND 9 developers and may be removed or changed in a future release.

-t *directory*

Chroot to *directory* after processing the command line arguments, but before reading the configuration file.

Warning: This option should be used in conjunction with the -u option, as chrooting a process running as root doesn't enhance security on most systems; the way chroot(2) is defined allows a process with root privileges to escape a chroot jail.

-u_*user*

Setuid to *user* after completing privileged operations, such as creating sockets that listen on privileged ports.

Note: On Linux, *named* uses the kernel's capability mechanism to drop all root privileges except the ability to bind(2) to a privileged port and set process resource limits. Unfortunately, this means that the -u option only works when *named* is run on kernel 2.2.18 or later, or kernel 2.3.99-pre3 or later, since previous kernels did not allow privileges to be retained after setuid(2).

-v

Report the version number and exit.

-x *cache-file* Load data from *cache-file* into the cache of the default view.

Warning: This option must not be used. It is only of interest to BIND 9 developers and may be removed or changed in a future release.

4.2. Signals

Certain UNIX signals cause the name server to take specific actions, as described in the following list. These signals can be sent to the *named* process using the kill command. The default process-id file is */var/run/named.pid.*

In routine operation, signals should not be used to control the nameserver; *rndc* should be used instead.

SIGHUP Causes the server to read *named.conf* and reload the database.

SIGTERM Causes the server to clean up and exit.

SIGINT Causes the server to clean up and exit.

The result of sending any other signals to the server is undefined.

4.3. rndc

The remote name daemon control (*rndc*) program allows the system administrator to control the operation of a name server. It supersedes the *ndc* utility that was provided in old BIND releases. Since BIND 9.2, *rndc* supports all the commands of the BIND 8 *ndc* utility except `ndc start` and `ndc restart`, which were also not supported in *ndc*'s channel mode. If *rndc* is invoked with no command line options or arguments, it prints a short summary of the supported commands and the available options and their arguments.

rndc communicates with the name server over a TCP connection, sending commands authenticated with digital signatures. In the current versions of *rndc* and *named*, the only supported authentication algorithm is HMAC-MD5, which uses a shared secret on each end of the connection. This provides TSIG-style authentication for the command request and the name server's response. All commands sent over the channel must be signed by a *key_id* known to the server. There is currently no way to provide the shared secret for a *key_id* without using the configuration file.

rndc reads a configuration file to determine how to contact the name server and decide what algorithm and key it should use.

```
rndc [-b source-address] [-c config-file] [-k key-file]
    [-s server] [-p port] [-V] [-y key_id] {command}
```

4.3.1. rndc Options

-b *source-address*

Use *source-address* as the source address for the connection to the server. Multiple instances are permitted to allow setting of both the IPv4 and IPv6 source addresses.

-c *config-file* Use *config-file* as the configuration file instead of the default, */etc/rndc.conf*.[2]

-k *key-file*

Use *key-file* as the key file instead of the default, */etc/rndc.key*. The key in */etc/rndc.key* will be used to authenticate commands sent to the server if the *config-file* does not exist.

-s *server*

server is the name or address of the server which matches a server statement in the configuration file for *rndc*. If no server is supplied on the command line, the host named by the **`default-server`** clause in the **`options`** statement of the *rndc* configuration file will be used.

-p *port*

Send commands to TCP port *port* instead of BIND 9's default control channel port, 953.

-V

Enable verbose logging.

-y *key_id*

Use the key *key_id* from the configuration file. *key_id* must be known by named with the same algorithm and secret string in order for control message validation to succeed. If no *key_id* is specified, *rndc* will first look for a key clause in the server statement of the server being used, or if no server statement is present for that host, then the default-key clause of the options statement. Note that the configuration file contains shared secrets which are used to send authenticated control commands to name servers. It should therefore not have general read or write access.

For the complete set of commands supported by *rndc*, run **`rndc`** without arguments to see its help message.

[2] See section 3.4 about locations of configuration files

4.3.2. rndc Commands

The command is one of the following:

dumpdb [-all|-cache|-zone] [view ...]

Dump the server's caches (default) and/or zones to the dump file for the specified views. If no view is specified, all views are dumped. This default file name is *named_dump.db*. The file name is defined with the **`dump-file`** option; see page 99 for details.

flush

Flushes the server's cache.

flushname *name*

Flushes the given name from the server's cache.

freeze [zone [class [view]]]

Suspend updates to a dynamic zone. If no zone is specified, then all zones are suspended. This allows manual edits to be made to a zone normally updated by dynamic update. It also causes changes in the journal file to be synced into the master and the journal file to be removed. All dynamic update attempts will be refused while the zone is frozen. (Also see **thaw**.)[3]

halt [-p]

Stop the server immediately. Recent changes made through dynamic update or IXFR are not saved to the master files, but will be rolled forward from the journal files when the server is restarted. If -p is specified *named*'s process id is returned. This allows an external process to determine when *named* had completed halting. (Also see **stop**.)

notify *zone [class [view]]*

Resend NOTIFY messages for the zone.

notrace

Sets the server's debugging level to 0.

[3] And see the example on page 56.

querylog

Toggle query logging. Query logging can also be enabled by explicitly directing the queries category to a channel in the logging section of *named.conf* or by specifying "`querylog yes;`" in the `options` section of *named.conf*. (See page 107 for details.)

reconfig

Reload the configuration file and load new zones, but do not reload existing zone files even if they have changed. This is faster than a full reload when there is a large number of zones because it avoids the need to examine the modification times of the zones files.

recursing

Dump the list of queries named is currently recursing on. The file name defaults to *named.recursing*. The file name is defined with the `recursing-file` option; see page 99 for details.

refresh zone [class [view]]

Schedule zone maintenance for the given zone.

reload

Reload configuration file and zones.

reload zone [class [view]]

Reload the given zone.

retransfer zone [class [view]]

Retransfer the given zone from the master.

stats

Write server statistics to the statistics file. (This is covered in section 10.24.)

status

Display status of the server. Note that the number of zones includes the internal bind/CH zone and the default ./IN hint zone if there is not an explicit root zone configured.

stop [-p]

Stop the server, making sure any recent changes made through dynamic update or IXFR are first saved to the master files of the updated zones. If -p is specified *named*'s process id is returned. This allows an external process to determine when *named* had completed stopping. (Also see **halt**.)

thaw *[zone [class [view]]]*

Enable updates to a frozen dynamic zone. If no zone is specified, then all frozen zones are enabled. This causes the server to reload the zone from disk, and re-enables dynamic updates after the load has completed. After a zone is thawed, dynamic updates will no longer be refused. (Also see **freeze**.)

trace

Increment the servers debugging level by one.

trace level

Sets the server's debugging level to an explicit value. (Also see **notrace**.)

4.4. rndc configuration

A configuration file is required, since all communication with the server is authenticated with digital signatures that rely on a shared secret, and there is no way to provide that secret other than with a configuration file. The default location for the *rndc* configuration file is */etc/rndc.conf*, but an alternate location can be specified with the -c option. If the configuration file is not found, *rndc* will also look in */etc/rndc.key* (or whatever *sysconfdir* was defined when the BIND build was configured). The *rndc.key* file is generated by running "**`rndc-confgen -a`**" as described in the section called *controls Statement Definition and Usage* on page 84.

The format of the configuration file is similar to that of *named.conf*, but limited to only four statements, the **`options`**, **`key`**, **`server`** and **`include`** statements. These statements are what associate the secret keys to the servers with which they are meant to be shared. The order of statements is not significant.

The options statement has three clauses: **default-server**, **default-key**, and **default-port**. **default-server** takes a host name or address argument and represents the server that will be contacted if no -s option is provided on the command line. **default-key** takes the name of a key as its argument, as defined by a **key** statement. **default-port** specifies the port to which *rndc* should connect if no port is given on the command line or in a server statement.

The **key** statement defines a key to be used by *rndc* when authenticating with named. Its syntax is identical to the key statement in *named.conf* (covered in section 10.4). The keyword **key** is followed by a key name, which must be a valid domain name, though it need not actually be hierarchical; thus, a string like "rndc_key" is a valid name. The key statement has two clauses: algorithm and secret. While the configuration parser will accept any string as the argument to algorithm, currently only the string "hmac-md5" has any meaning. The secret is a base-64 encoded string as specified in RFC 3548.

The **server** statement associates a key defined using the **key** statement with a server. The keyword **server** is followed by a host name or address. The **server** statement has two clauses: **key** and **port**. The **key** clause specifies the name of the key to be used when communicating with this server, and the **port** clause can be used to specify the port *rndc* should connect to on the server.

A sample minimal configuration file is as follows:

```
key rndc_key {
     algorithm "hmac-md5";
     secret
     "c3Ryb25nIGVub3VnaCBmb3IgYSBtYW4gYnV0IG1hZGUgZm9yIGEgd29tYW4K";
};
options {
     default-server 127.0.0.1;
     default-key rndc_key;
};
```

This file, if installed as */etc/rndc.conf*, would allow the command:

```
$ rndc reload
```

to connect to 127.0.0.1 port 953 and cause the name server to reload, if a name server on the local machine were running with following controls statements:

```
controls {
     inet 127.0.0.1 allow { localhost; }
          keys { rndc_key; };
};
```

and it had an identical **key** statement for *rndc_key*.

4.5. rndc-confgen

The *rndc* key generation tool, *rndc-confgen,* generates configuration files for *rndc*. It can be used as a convenient alternative to writing the *rndc.conf* file and the corresponding **controls** and **key** statements in *named.conf* by hand. Alternatively, it can be run with the **-a** option to set up a *rndc.key* file and avoid the need for a *rndc.conf* file and a **controls** statement altogether.

```
rndc-confgen [-a] [-b keysize] [-c keyfile] [-h]
  [-k keyname] [-p port] [-r randomfile] [-s address]
  [-t chrootdir] [-u user]
```

rndc-confgen Command-line Options

-a

Do automatic *rndc* configuration. This creates a file *rndc.key* in */etc* (or whatever sysconfdir was specified as when BIND was built) that is read by both *rndc* and *named* on startup. The *rndc.key* file defines a default command channel and authentication key allowing *rndc* to communicate with *named* on the local host with no further configuration.

Running **rndc-confgen -a** allows BIND 9 and *rndc* to be used as drop-in replacements for BIND 8 and *ndc*, with no changes to the existing BIND 8 named.conf file.

If a more elaborate configuration than that generated by **rndc-confgen -a** is required, for example if *rndc* is to be used remotely, you should run **rndc-confgen** without the -a option and set up a *rndc.conf* and *named.conf* as directed.

-b *keysize* Specifies the size of the authentication key in bits. Must be between 1 and 512 bits; the default is 128.

-c *keyfile* Used with the -a option to specify an alternate location for *rndc.key*.

-h

Prints a short summary of the options and arguments to *rndc-confgen.*

-k *keyname* Specifies the key name of the rndc authentication key. This must be a valid domain name. The default is *rndc-key.*

-p *port* Specifies the command channel port where *named* listens for connections from *rndc*. The default is 953.

-r *randomfile*

Specifies a source of random data for generating the authorization. If the operating system does not provide a */dev/random* or equivalent device, the default source of randomness is keyboard input. *randomdev* specifies the name of a character device or file containing random data to be used instead of the default. The special value *keyboard* indicates that keyboard input should be used.

-s *address* Specifies the IP address where *named* listens for command channel connections from *rndc*. The default is the loopback address 127.0.0.1.

-t *chrootdir*

Used with the -a option to specify a directory where *named* will run chrooted. An additional copy of the *rndc.key* will be written relative to this directory so that it will be found by the chrooted *named*.

-u *user* Used with the -a option to set the owner of the *rndc.key* file generated. If -t is also specified only the file in the chroot area has its owner changed.

rndc-confgen Examples

To allow *rndc* to be used with no manual configuration, run:

```
rndc-confgen -a
```

To print a sample *rndc.conf* file and corresponding **controls** and **key** statements to be manually inserted into *named.conf*, run:

```
rndc-confgen
```

5. Administrative Tools

Administrative tools play an integral part in the management of a server. This chapter covers the following tools: *named-checkconf*, *named-checkzone*, *named-compilezone*, *nsupdate*, *dnssec-keygen*, and *dnssec-signzone*.[1]

Note: The *dnssec-keygen* and *dnssec-signzone* tools now provide alternative functionality for *dnssec-signkey* and *dnssec-makekeyset*.

5.1. named-checkconf

The *named-checkconf* program checks the syntax, but not the semantics, of a *named.conf* file. It prints errors to the console. It returns an exit status of 1 if errors were detected and 0 otherwise.

```
named-checkconf [-jhvz] [-t directory] [filename]
```

The options are:

-h

Print the usage summary and exit. (This option was introduced in BIND 9.5.)

-t directory

Chroot to *directory* so that include directives in the configuration file are processed as if run by a similarly chrooted *named*.

-v

Print the version of the *named-checkconf* program and exit.

-z

Perform a test load of all the master zones found in *named.conf*.

-j

When loading a zonefile read the journal if it exists.

filename

The name of the configuration file to be checked. If not specified, it defaults to */etc/named.conf*.

[1]The *rndc* command and the *named* server are covered in chapter 4.

named-checkconf Example

```
# named-checkconf named.conf
named.conf:13: unknown option 'allow-query-cche'
named.conf:29: unexpected token near '}'
```

5.2. named-checkzone

The *named-checkzone* program checks a master file for syntax and consistency.

```
named-checkzone [-dhjqvD] [-c class] [-o output]
   [-t directory] [-f format] [-F format] [-i mode]
   [-w directory] [-k (ignore|warn|fail)] [-m mode]
   [-M mode] [-n (ignore|warn|fail)] [-o filename]
   [-s style] [-S mode] [-t directory] -W (ignore|warn)
   zonename [filename]
```

named-checkzone performs the same checks as *named* does when loading a zone. This makes *named-checkzone* useful for checking zone files before configuring them into a name server.

named-checkzone returns an exit status of 1 if errors were detected and 0 otherwise.

Options for named-checkzone and named-compilezone

-d

Enable debugging.

-h

Print the usage summary and exit. (This option was added in BIND 9.5.)

-q

Quiet mode - exit code only.

-v

Print the version of the *named-checkzone* program and exit.

-j

When loading the zone file read the journal if it exists.

-c *class* Specify the class of the zone. If not specified “IN” is assumed.

-i *mode*

Perform post-load zone integrity checks. Possible modes are "*full*" (default), "*full-sibling*", "*local*", "*local-sibling*" and "*none*" .

Mode "*full*" checks that MX records refer to A or AAAA record (both in-zone and out-of-zone hostnames). Mode "*local*" only checks MX records which refer to in-zone hostnames.

Mode "*full*" checks that SRV records refer to A or AAAA record (both in-zone and out-of-zone hostnames). Mode **"local"** only checks SRV records which refer to in-zone hostnames.

Mode "*full*" checks that delegation NS records refer to A or AAAA record (both in-zone and out-of-zone hostnames). It also checks that glue address records in the zone match those advertised by the child. Mode "*local*" only checks NS records which refer to in-zone hostnames or that some required glue exists, that is when the nameserver is in a child zone.

Mode "*full-sibling*" and "*local-sibling*" disable sibling glue checks but are otherwise the same as "*full*" and "*local*" respectively.

Mode "*none*" disables the checks.

-f *format* Specify the format of the zone file. Possible formats are "*text*" (default) and "*raw*" .

-F *format*

Specify the format of the output file specified. Possible formats are "*text*" (default) and "*raw*". For *named-checkzone*, this does not cause any effects unless it dumps the zone contents.

-k *mode*

Perform "*check-names*" checks with the specified failure mode. Possible modes are "*fail*" (default for *named-compilezone*), "*warn*" (default for *named-checkzone*) and "*ignore*". (See page 107 about the **check-names** option for more details.)

-m *mode*

Specify whether MX records should be checked to see if they are addresses. Possible modes are "*fail*", "*warn*" (default) and "*ignore*".

-M *mode*

Check if a MX record refers to a CNAME. Possible modes are "*fail*" , "*warn*" (default) and "*ignore*".

-n *mode* Specify whether NS records should be checked to see if they are addresses. Possible modes are "*fail*" (default for *named-compilezone*), "*warn*" (default for *named-checkzone*) and "*ignore*".

-o *filename* Write zone output to *filename*. If *filename* is - (dash) then write to standard out. This is mandatory for *named-compilezone*.

-s *style*

Specify the style of the dumped zone file. Possible styles are "*full*" (default) and "*relative*". The full format is most suitable for processing automatically by a separate script. On the other hand, the relative format is more human-readable and is thus suitable for editing by hand. For *named-checkzone*, this does not cause any effects unless it dumps the zone contents. It also does not have any meaning if the output format is not text.

-S *mode*

Check if a SRV record refers to a CNAME. Possible modes are "*fail*", "*warn*" (default) and "*ignore*".

-t *directory*

Chroot to *directory* so that include directives in the configuration file are processed as if run by a similarly chrooted named.

-w *directory*

chdir to *directory* so that relative filenames in master file **$INCLUDE** directives work. This is similar to the directory clause in *named.conf*.

-D

Dump zone file in canonical format. This is always enabled for named-compilezone.

-W *mode*

Specify whether to check for non-terminal wildcards. Non-terminal wildcards are almost always the result of a failure to understand the wildcard matching algorithm (RFC 1034). Possible modes are "*warn*" (default) and "*ignore*".

zonename

The domain name of the zone being checked.

filename

The name of the zone file.

named-checkzone Example

```
# named-checkzone example.org /etc/named/e/ex/example.org
/etc/named/e/ex/example.org:29: warning: '192.168.130.29': ⇓
  MX is an address
zone example.org/IN: example.org/MX 'mail.example.org' is a ⇓
```

```
 CNAME (illegal)
zone example.org/IN: loaded serial 2007072625
OK
```

5.3. named-compilezone

Similar to *named-checkzone*, but it always dumps the zone content to a specified file (typically in a different format). Additionally, it applies stricter check levels by default, since the dump output will be used as an actual zone file loaded by *named*. When manually specified otherwise, the check levels must at least be as strict as those specified in the *named* configuration file.

```
named-compilezone [-d] [-j] [-q] [-v] [-c class] [-C mode]
   [-f format] [-F format] [-i mode] [-k mode] [-m mode]
   [-n mode] [-o filename] [-s style] [-t directory]
   [-w directory] [-D] [-W mode] {zonename} {filename}
```

See the *named-checkzone* options starting on page 26 for details.

5.4. nsupdate

The *nsupdate* tool is used to submit Dynamic DNS Update requests as defined in RFC 2136 to a name server. This allows resource records to be added or removed from a zone without manually editing the zone file. A single update request can contain requests to add or remove more than one resource record.

Zones that are under dynamic control via *nsupdate* or a DHCP server should not be edited by hand. Manual edits could conflict with dynamic updates and cause data to be lost.

The resource records that are dynamically added or removed with *nsupdate* have to be in the same zone. Requests are sent to the zone's master server. This is identified by the MNAME field of the zone's SOA record.

```
nsupdate [-d] [[-y [hmac:]keyname:secret] | [-k keyfile]]
  [-t timeout] [-u udptimeout] [-r udpretries] [-v] [filename]
```

The -d option makes *nsupdate* operate in debug mode. This provides tracing information about the update requests that are made and the replies received from the name server.

Transaction signatures can be used to authenticate the Dynamic DNS updates. These use the TSIG resource record type described in RFC 2845 or the SIG(0) record described in RFC 3535 and RFC 2931. TSIG relies on a shared secret that should only be known to *nsupdate* and the name server. Currently, the only supported encryption algorithm for TSIG is HMAC-MD5, which is defined in RFC 2104. Once other algorithms are defined for TSIG, applications will need to ensure they select the appropriate algorithm as well as the key when authenticating each other. For instance, suitable key and server statements would be added to */etc/named.conf* so that the name server can associate the appropriate secret key and algorithm with the IP address of the client application that will be using TSIG authentication. SIG(0) uses public key cryptography. To use a SIG(0) key, the public key must be stored in a KEY record in a zone served by the name server. *nsupdate* does not read */etc/named.conf*.

nsupdate uses the -y or -k option to provide the shared secret needed to generate a TSIG record for authenticating Dynamic DNS update requests, default type HMAC-MD5. These options are mutually exclusive. With the -k option, *nsupdate* reads the shared secret from the file *keyfile*, whose name is of the form *K{name}.+157.+{random}.private*. For historical reasons, the file *K{name}.+157.+{random}.key* must also be present.[2] When the -y option is used, a signature is generated from [*hmac:*]*keyname:secret*. *keyname* is the name of the key, and *secret* is the base64 encoded shared secret. Use of the -y option is discouraged because the shared secret is supplied as a command line argument in clear text. This may be visible in the output from ps(1) or in a history file maintained by the user's shell.

The -k may also be used to specify a SIG(0) key used to authenticate Dynamic DNS update requests. In this case, the key specified is not an HMAC-MD5 key.

By default, *nsupdate* uses UDP to send update requests to the name server unless they are too large to fit in a UDP request in which case TCP will be used. The -v option makes *nsupdate* use a TCP connection. This may be preferable when a batch of update requests is made.

The -t option sets the maximum time an update request can take before it is aborted. The default is 300 seconds. Zero can be used to disable the timeout.

The -u option sets the UDP retry interval. The default is 3 seconds. If zero, the interval will be computed from the timeout interval and number of UDP retries.

The -r option sets the number of UDP retries. The default is 3. If zero, only one update request will be made.

Input format for nsupdate

nsupdate reads input from *filename* or standard input. Each command is supplied on exactly one line of input. Some commands are for administrative purposes. The others are either update instructions or prerequisite checks on the contents of the zone. These checks set conditions that some name or set of resource records (RRset) either exists

[2] The TSIG key is redundantly stored in two separate files. This is a consequence of *nsupdate* using the DST library for its cryptographic operations, and may change in future releases.

or is absent from the zone. These conditions must be met if the entire update request is to succeed. Updates will be rejected if the tests for the prerequisite conditions fail.

Every update request consists of zero or more prerequisites and zero or more updates. This allows a suitably authenticated update request to proceed if some specified resource records are present or missing from the zone. A blank input line (or the **send** command) causes the accumulated commands to be sent as one Dynamic DNS update request to the name server.

The command formats and their meaning are as follows:

answer

Displays the answer.

class {*classname*}

Specify the default class. If no *class* is specified, the default class is *IN*.

local {*address*} [*port*]

Sends all dynamic update requests using the local *address*. When no local statement is provided, *nsupdate* will send updates using an address and port chosen by the system. *port* can additionally be used to make requests come from a specific port. If no port number is specified, the system will assign one.

key {*name*} {*secret*}

Specifies that all updates are to be TSIG-signed using the *keyname keysecret* pair. The **key** command overrides any key specified on the command line via -y or -k.

prereq nxdomain {*domain-name*}

Requires that no resource record of any type exists with name *domain-name*.

prereq yxdomain {*domain-name*}

Requires that *domain-name* exists (has as at least one resource record, of any type).

prereq nxrrset {*domain-name*} [*class* {*type*}]

Requires that no resource record exists of the specified *type*, *class* and *domain-name*. If *class* is omitted, IN (internet) is assumed.

prereq yxrrset {*domain-name*} [*class* {*type*}]

This requires that a resource record of the specified *type*, *class* and *domain-name* must exist. If *class* is omitted, IN (internet) is assumed.

prereq yxrrset {*domain-name*} [*class* {*type*} {*data...*}]

The *data* from each set of prerequisites of this form sharing a common *type*, *class*, and *domain-name* are combined to form a set of RRs. This set of RRs must exactly match the set of RRs existing in the zone at the given *type*, *class*, and *domain-name*. The *data* are written in the standard text representation of the resource record's RDATA.

send Sends the current message. This is equivalent to entering a blank line.

server {*servername*} [*port*]

Sends all dynamic update requests to the name server *servername*. When no server statement is provided, *nsupdate* will send updates to the master server of the correct zone. The MNAME field of that zone's SOA record will identify the master server for that zone. *port* is the port number on *servername* where the dynamic update requests get sent. If no port number is specified, the default DNS port number of 53 is used.

show

Displays the current message, containing all of the prerequisites and updates specified since the last send.

update add {*domain-name*} {*ttl*} [*class* {*type*} {*data...*}]

Adds a new resource record with the specified *ttl*, *class* and *data*.

update delete {*domain-name*} [*ttl* [*class*] [*type* [*data...*]]]

Deletes any resource records named *domain-name*. If *type* and *data* is provided, only matching resource records will be removed. The internet class is assumed if *class* is not supplied. The *ttl* is ignored, and is only allowed for compatibility.

zone {*zonename*}

Specifies that all updates are to be made to the zone *zonename*. If no *zone* statement is provided, *nsupdate* will attempt determine the correct zone to update based on the rest of the input.

Lines beginning with a semicolon are comments and are ignored.

nsupdate Examples

The examples below show how *nsupdate* could be used to insert and delete resource records from the example.com zone. Notice that the input in each example contains a trailing blank line so that a group of commands are sent as one dynamic update request to the master name server for *example.com*.

```
# nsupdate
> update delete oldhost.example.com A
> update add newhost.example.com 86400 A 172.16.1.1
> send
```

Any A records for *oldhost.example.com* are deleted. And an A record for *newhost.example.com* with IP address 172.16.1.1 is added. The newly-added record has a one day TTL (86400 seconds).

```
# nsupdate
> prereq nxdomain nickname.example.com
> update add nickname.example.com 86400 CNAME ⇓
 somehost.example.com
> send
```

The prerequisite condition gets the name server to check that there are no resource records of any type for nickname.example.com. If there are, the update request fails. If this name does not exist, a CNAME for it is added. This ensures that when the CNAME is added, it cannot conflict with the long-standing rule in RFC 1034 that a name must not exist as any other record type if it exists as a CNAME. (The rule has been updated for DNSSEC in RFC 2535 to allow CNAMEs to have RRSIG, DNSKEY and NSEC records.)

5.5. dnssec-keygen

The *dnssec-keygen* tool generates keys for DNSSEC (Secure DNS), as defined in RFC 2535 and RFC 4034. It can also generate keys for use with TSIG (Transaction Signatures), as defined in RFC 2845.

```
dnssec-keygen {-a algorithm} {-b keysize} {-n nametype}
  [-c class] [-e] [-f flag] [-g generator] [-h] [-k]
  [-p protocol] [-r randomdev] [-s strength] [-t type]
  [-v level] {name}
```

dnssec-keygen Options

-a *algorithm*

Selects the cryptographic algorithm. The value of *algorithm* must be one of RSAMD5 (RSA) or RSASHA1, DSA, DH (Diffie Hellman), or HMAC-MD5. These values are case insensitive.

Note 1: that for DNSSEC, RSASHA1 is a mandatory to implement algorithm, and DSA is recommended. For TSIG, HMAC-MD5 is mandatory.

Note 2: HMAC-MD5 and DH automatically set the -k flag.

-b *keysize* Specifies the number of bits in the key. The choice of key size depends on the algorithm used. RSAMD5 / RSASHA1 keys must be between 512 and 2048 bits. Diffie Hellman keys must be between 128 and 4096 bits. DSA keys must be between 512 and 1024 bits and an exact multiple of 64. HMAC-MD5 keys must be between 1 and 512 bits.

-n *nametype* Specifies the owner type of the key. The value of *nametype* must either be ZONE (for a DNSSEC zone key (KEY/DNSKEY)), HOST or ENTITY (for a key associated with a host (KEY)), USER (for a key associated with a user(KEY)) or OTHER (DNSKEY). These values are case insensitive. Defaults to ZONE for DNSKEY generation.

-c *class* Indicates that the DNS record containing the key should have the specified *class*. If not specified, class IN is used.

-e

If generating an RSAMD5/RSASHA1 key, use a large exponent.

-f *flag* Set the specified *flag* in the flag field of the KEY/DNSKEY record. The only recognized flag is KSK (Key Signing Key) DNSKEY.

-g *generator* If generating a Diffie Hellman key, use this *generator*. Allowed values are 2 and 5. If no generator is specified, a known prime from RFC 2539 will be used if possible; otherwise the default is 2.

-h

Prints a short summary of the options and arguments to *dnssec-keygen*.

-k

Generate KEY records rather than DNSKEY records.

-p *protocol* Sets the protocol value for the generated key. The *protocol* is a number between 0 and 255. The default is 3 (DNSSEC). Other possible values for this argument are listed in RFC 2535 and its successors.

-r *randomdev*

Specifies the source of randomness. If the operating system does not provide a */dev/random* or equivalent device, the default source of randomness is keyboard input. *randomdev* specifies the name of a character device or file containing random data to be used instead of the default. The special value *keyboard* indicates that keyboard input should be used.

-s *strength* Specifies the strength value of the key. The *strength* is a number between 0 and 15, and currently has no defined purpose in DNSSEC.

-t *type*

Indicates the use of the key. *type* must be one of AUTHCONF, NOAUTHCONF, NOAUTH, or NOCONF. The default is AUTHCONF. AUTH refers to the ability to authenticate data, and CONF the ability to encrypt data.

-v *level*

Sets the debugging level.

Generated keys

When *dnssec-keygen* completes successfully, it prints a string of the form *Knnnn.+aaa+iiiii* to the standard output. This is an identification string for the key it has generated.

nnnn is the key name.

aaa is the numeric representation of the algorithm.

iiiii is the key identifier (or footprint).

dnssec-keygen creates two files, with names based on the printed string: *Knnnn.+aaa+iiiii.key* contains the public key, and *Knnnn.+aaa+iiiii.private* contains the private key.

The .key file contains a DNS KEY record that can be inserted into a zone file (directly or with a **$INCLUDE** statement).

The .private file contains algorithm-specific fields. For obvious security reasons, this file does not have general read permission.

Both .key and .private files are generated for symmetric encryption algorithms such as HMAC-MD5, even though the public and private key are equivalent.

Example of using dnssec-keygen

To generate a 768-bit DSA key for the domain *example.com*, the following command would be issued:

```
dnssec-keygen -a DSA -b 768 -n ZONE example.com
```

The command would print a string of the form:

```
Kexample.com.+003+26160
```

In this example, *dnssec-keygen* creates the files *Kexample.com.+003+26160.key* and *Kexample.com.+003+26160.private*.

5.6. dnssec-signzone

The *dnssec-signzone* tool signs a zone. It generates NSEC and RRSIG records and produces a signed version of the zone. The security status of delegations from the signed zone (that is, whether the child zones are secure or not) is determined by the presence or absence of a keyset file for each child zone.

```
dnssec-signzone [-a] [-c class] [-d directory] [-e end-time]
  [-f output-file] [-g] [-h] [-k key] [-l domain] [-i interval]
  [-I input-format] [-j jitter] [-N soa-serial-format]
  [-o origin] [-O output-format] [-p] [-r randomdev]
  [-s start-time] [-t] [-v level] [-z] {zonefile} [key...]
```

dnssec-signzone Options

-a

Verify all generated signatures.

-c *class*

Specifies the DNS class of the zone.

-k *key* Treat specified *key* as a key signing key ignoring any key flags. This option may be specified multiple times.

-l *domain* Generate a DLV set in addition to the key (DNSKEY) and DS sets. The *domain* is appended to the name of the records.

-d *directory* Look for keyset files in *directory* as the directory

-g

Generate DS records for child zones from keyset files. Existing DS records will be removed.

-s *start-time*

Specify the date and time when the generated RRSIG records become valid. This can be either an absolute or relative time. An absolute start time is indicated by a number in *YYYYMMDDHHMMSS* notation; 20000530144500 denotes 14:45:00 UTC on May 30th, 2000. A relative start time is indicated by +*N*, which is *N* seconds from the current time. If no *start-time* is specified, the current time minus 1 hour (to allow for clock skew) is used.

-e *end-time* Specify the date and time when the generated RRSIG records expire. As with start-time, an absolute time is indicated in *YYYYMMDDHHMMSS* notation. A time relative to the start time is indicated with +*N*, which is *N* seconds from the start time. A time relative to the current time is indicated with now+*N*. If no *end-time* is specified, 30 days from the start time is used as a default.

-f *output-file*

The name of the output file containing the signed zone. The default is to append *.signed* to the input filename.

-h

Prints a short summary of the options and arguments to *dnssec-signzone*.

-i *interval*

When a previously-signed zone is passed as input, records may be resigned. The interval option specifies the cycle interval as an offset from the current time (in seconds). If a RRSIG record expires after the cycle interval, it is retained. Otherwise, it is considered to be expiring soon, and it will be replaced.

The default cycle interval is one quarter of the difference between the signature end and start times. So if neither end-time or start-time are specified, *dnssec-signzone* generates signatures that are valid for 30 days, with a cycle interval of 7.5 days. Therefore, if any existing RRSIG records are due to expire in less than 7.5 days, they would be replaced.

-I *input-format* The format of the input zone file. Possible formats are "*text*" (default) and "*raw*". This option is primarily intended to be used for dynamic signed zones so that the dumped zone file in a non-text format containing updates can be signed directly. The use of this option does not make much sense for non-dynamic zones.

-j *jitter*

When signing a zone with a fixed signature lifetime, all RRSIG records issued at the time of signing expires simultaneously. If the zone is incrementally signed, i.e. a previously-signed zone is passed as input to the signer, all expired signatures have to be regenerated at about the same time. The *jitter* option specifies a jitter window that will be used to randomize the signature expire time, thus spreading incremental signature regeneration over time.

Signature lifetime jitter also to some extent benefits validators and servers by spreading out cache expiration, i.e. if large numbers of RRSIGs don't expire at the same time from all caches there will be less congestion than if all validators need to refetch at mostly the same time.

-n *ncpus*

Specifies the number of threads to use. By default, one thread is started for each detected CPU.

-N *soa-serial-format* The SOA serial number format of the signed zone. Possible formats are "*keep*" (default), "*increment*" and "*unixtime*".

keep

Do not modify the SOA serial number.

increment

Increment the SOA serial number using RFC 1982 arithmetics.

unixtime Set the SOA serial number to the number of seconds since epoch.

-o *origin*

The zone origin. If not specified, the name of the zone file is assumed to be the origin.

-O *output-format* The format of the output file containing the signed zone. Possible formats are "*text*" (default) and "*raw*".

-p

Use pseudo-random data when signing the zone. This is faster, but less secure, than using real random data. This option may be useful when signing large zones or when the entropy source is limited.

-r *randomdev*

Specifies the source of randomness. If the operating system does not provide a */dev/random* or equivalent device, the default source of randomness is keyboard input. *randomdev* specifies the name of a character device or file containing random data to be used instead of the default. The special value keyboard indicates that keyboard input should be used.

-t

Print statistics at completion.

-v *level* Sets the debugging level.

-z

Ignore KSK flag on key when determining what to sign.

zonefile

The file containing the zone to be signed.

key

Specify which keys should be used to sign the zone. If no keys are specified, then the zone will be examined for DNSKEY records at the zone apex. If these are found and there are matching private keys, in the current directory, then these will be used for signing.

Example of using dnssec-signzone

The following command signs the *example.com* zone with the DSA key generated by dnssec-keygen (*Kexample.com.+003+17247*). The zone's keys must be in the master file (*db.example.com* in this example). This invocation looks for keyset files, in the current directory, so that DS records can be generated from them (-g).

```
% dnssec-signzone -g -o example.com db.example.com \
  Kexample.com.+003+17247
db.example.com.signed
```

In the above example, *dnssec-signzone* creates the file *db.example.com.signed*. This should be referenced in a zone statement in a named.conf file.

This example re-signs a previously-signed zone with default parameters. The private keys are assumed to be in the current directory.

```
% cp db.example.com.signed db.example.com
% dnssec-signzone -o example.com db.example.com
db.example.com.signed
```

6. Diagnostic Tools

This chapter describes the command-line *dig*, *host*, and *nslookup* programs for manually querying name servers. They differ in style and output format.

6.1. dig

The domain information groper (*dig*) is the most versatile and complete of these lookup tools. It has two modes: simple interactive mode for a single query, and batch mode which executes a query for each in a list of several query lines. All query options are accessible from the command line.

```
dig [@server] [-b address] [-c class] [-f filename]
  [-k filename] [-p port#] [-q name] [-t type] [-x addr]
  [-y [hmac:]name:key] [-4] [-6] [name] [type] [class]
  [queryopt...]
```

```
dig [-h]
```

```
dig [global-queryopt...] [query...]
```

dig is a flexible tool for interrogating DNS name servers. It performs DNS lookups and displays the answers that are returned from the name server(s) that were queried. Most DNS administrators use *dig* to troubleshoot DNS problems because of its flexibility, ease of use and clarity of output. Other lookup tools tend to have less functionality than *dig*.

The verbose output from *dig* is in zone file format. Extra details are commented using semicolons.

Although *dig* is normally used with command-line arguments, it also has a batch mode of operation for reading lookup requests from a file. A brief summary of its command-line arguments and options is printed when the -h option is given. Unlike earlier versions, the BIND 9 implementation of *dig* allows multiple lookups to be issued from the command line.

Unless it is told to query a specific name server, *dig* will try each of the servers listed in */etc/resolv.conf*.

When no command line arguments or options are given, will perform an NS query for "." (the root).

It is possible to set per-user defaults for *dig* via *${HOME}/.digrc*. This file is read and any options in it are applied before the command line arguments.

The IN and CH class names overlap with the IN and CH top level domains names. Either use the -t and -c options to specify the type and class or use the -q the specify the domain name or use "IN." and "CH." when looking up these top level domains.

6.1.1. Simple dig Usage

A typical invocation of **dig** looks like:

```
dig @server name type
```

Where:

server

is the name or IP address of the name server to query. This can be an IPv4 address in dotted-decimal notation or an IPv6 address in colon-delimited notation. When the supplied *server* argument is a hostname, *dig* resolves that name before querying that name server. If no *server* argument is provided, *dig* consults */etc/resolv.conf* and queries the name servers listed there. The reply from the name server that responds is displayed.

name

is the name of the resource record that is to be looked up.

type

indicates what type of query is required – ANY, A, MX, SIG, etc. *type* can be any valid query type. If no *type* argument is supplied, *dig* will perform a lookup for an A record.

6.1.2. Options for dig

The -b option sets the source IP address of the query to *address*. This must be a valid address on one of the host's network interfaces or "0.0.0.0" or "::". An optional port may be specified by appending "#<port>"

The default query class (IN for internet) is overridden by the -c option. *class* is any valid class, such as HS for Hesiod records or CH for Chaosnet records.

The -f option makes *dig* operate in batch mode by reading a list of lookup requests to process from the file *filename*. The file contains a number of queries, one per line.

Each entry in the file should be organized in the same way they would be presented as queries to *dig* using the command-line interface.

If a non-standard port number is to be queried, the -p option is used. *port#* is the port number that *dig* will send its queries instead of the standard DNS port number 53. This option would be used to test a name server that has been configured to listen for queries on a non-standard port number.

The -4 option forces *dig* to only use IPv4 query transport. The -6 option forces *dig* to only use IPv6 query transport.

The -t option sets the query type to *type*. It can be any valid query type which is supported in BIND 9. The default query type is"A", unless the -x option is supplied to indicate a reverse lookup. A zone transfer can be requested by specifying a type of AXFR. When an incremental zone transfer (IXFR) is required, *type* is set to ixfr=N. The incremental zone transfer will contain the changes made to the zone since the serial number in the zone's SOA record was *N*.

The -q option sets the query name to *name*. This useful do distinguish the *name* from other arguments.

Reverse lookups – mapping addresses to names – are simplified by the -x option. *addr* is an IPv4 address in dotted-decimal notation, or a colon-delimited IPv6 address. When this option is used, there is no need to provide the *name*, *class* and *type* arguments. *dig* automatically performs a lookup for a name like 11.12.13.10.in-addr.arpa and sets the query type and class to PTR and IN respectively. By default, IPv6 addresses are looked up using nibble format under the IP6.ARPA domain. To use the older RFC 1886 method using the IP6.INT domain specify the -i option. Bit string labels (RFC 2874) are now experimental and are not attempted.

To sign the DNS queries sent by *dig* and their responses using transaction signatures (TSIG), specify a TSIG key file using the -k option. You can also specify the TSIG key itself on the command line using the -y option; *hmac* is the type of the TSIG, default HMAC-MD5, *name* is the name of the TSIG key and *key* is the actual key. The key is a base-64 encoded string, typically generated by dnssec-keygen(8). Caution should be taken when using the -y option on multi-user systems as the key can be visible in the output from ps(1) or in the shell's history file. When using TSIG authentication with *dig*, the name server that is queried needs to know the key and algorithm that is being used. In BIND, this is done by providing appropriate **key** and **server** statements in named.conf.

6.1.3. Query Options for dig

dig provides a number of query options[1] which affect the way in which lookups are made and the results displayed. Some of these set or reset flag bits in the query header, some determine which sections of the answer get printed, and others determine the timeout and retry strategies.

[1]There are probably too many query options.

Each query option is identified by a keyword preceded by a plus sign (+). Some keywords set or reset an option. These may be preceded by the string no to negate the meaning of that keyword. Other keywords assign values to options like the timeout interval. They have the form *+keyword=value*. The query options are:

+[no]tcp

Use [do not use] TCP when querying name servers. The default behavior is to use UDP unless an AXFR or IXFR query is requested, in which case a TCP connection is used.

+[no]vc

Use [do not use] TCP when querying name servers. This alternate syntax to *+[no]tcp* is provided for backwards compatibility. The "vc" stands for "virtual circuit".

+[no]ignore

Ignore truncation in UDP responses instead of retrying with TCP. By default, TCP retries are performed.

+domain=somename

Set the search list to contain the single domain *somename*, as if specified in a **domain** directive in */etc/resolv.conf*, and enable search list processing as if the *+search* option were given.

+[no]search

Use [do not use] the search list defined by the searchlist or domain directive in resolv.conf (if any). The search list is not used by default.

+[no]showsearch

Perform [do not perform] a search showing intermediate results.

+[no]defname

Deprecated, treated as a synonym for *+[no]search*

+[no]aaonly

Sets the "aa" flag in the query.

+[no]aaflag

A synonym for *+[no]aaonly*.

+[no]adflag

Set [do not set] the AD (authentic data) bit in the query. The AD bit currently has a standard meaning only in responses, not in queries, but the ability to set the bit in the query is provided for completeness.

+[no]cdflag

Set [do not set] the CD (checking disabled) bit in the query. This requests the server to not perform DNSSEC validation of responses.

+[no]cl

Display [do not display] the CLASS when printing the record.

+[no]ttlid

Display [do not display] the TTL when printing the record.

+[no]recurse

Toggle the setting of the RD (recursion desired) bit in the query. This bit is set by default, which means *dig* normally sends recursive queries. Recursion is automatically disabled when the *+nssearch* or *+trace* query options are used.

+[no]nssearch

When this option is set, *dig* attempts to find the authoritative name servers for the zone containing the name being looked up and display the SOA record that each name server has for the zone.

+[no]trace

Toggle tracing of the delegation path from the root name servers for the name being looked up. Tracing is disabled by default. When tracing is enabled, *dig* makes iterative queries to resolve the name being looked up. It will follow referrals from the root servers, showing the answer from each server that was used to resolve the lookup.

+[no]cmd

Toggles the printing of the initial comment in the output identifying the version of *dig* and the query options that have been applied. This comment is printed by default.

+[no]short

Provide a terse answer. The default is to print the answer in a verbose form.

+[no]identify

Show [or do not show] the IP address and port number that supplied the answer when the *+short* option is enabled. If short form answers are requested, the default is not to show the source address and port number of the server that provided the answer.

+[no]comments

Toggle the display of comment lines in the output. The default is to print comments.

+[no]stats

This query option toggles the printing of statistics: when the query was made, the size of the reply and so on. The default behavior is to print the query statistics.

+[no]qr

Print [do not print] the query as it is sent. By default, the query is not printed.

+[no]question

Print [do not print] the question section of a query when an answer is returned. The default is to print the question section as a comment.

+[no]answer

Display [do not display] the answer section of a reply. The default is to display it.

+[no]authority

Display [do not display] the authority section of a reply. The default is to display it.

+[no]additional

Display [do not display] the additional section of a reply. The default is to display it.

+[no]all

Set or clear all display flags.

+time=*T*

Sets the timeout for a query to *T* seconds. The default timeout is 5 seconds. An attempt to set *T* to less than 1 will result in a query timeout of 1 second being applied.

+tries=*T*

Sets the number of times to try UDP queries to server to *T* instead of the default, 3. If *T* is less than or equal to zero, the number of tries is silently rounded up to 1.

+retry=*T*

Sets the number of times to retry UDP queries to server to *T* instead of the default, 2. Unlike *+tries*, this does not include the initial query.

+ndots=*D*

Set the number of dots that have to appear in *name* to *D* for it to be considered absolute. The default value is that defined using the ndots statement in */etc/resolv.conf*, or 1 if no ndots statement is present. Names with fewer dots are interpreted as relative names and will be searched for in the domains listed in the search or domain directive in */etc/resolv.conf*.

+bufsize=*B*

Set the UDP message buffer size advertised using EDNS0 to *B* bytes. The maximum and minimum sizes of this buffer are 65535 and 0 respectively. Values outside this range are rounded up or down appropriately. Values other than zero will cause a EDNS query to be sent.

+edns=#

Specify the EDNS version to query with. Valid values are 0 to 255. Setting the EDNS version will cause a EDNS query to be sent. +noedns clears the remembered EDNS version.

+[no]multiline

Print records like the SOA records in a verbose multi-line format with human-readable comments. The default is to print each record on a single line, to facilitate machine parsing of the *dig* output.

+[no]fail

Do not try the next server if you receive a SERVFAIL. The default is to not try the next server which is the reverse of normal stub resolver behavior.

+[no]besteffort

Attempt to display the contents of messages which are malformed. The default is to not display malformed answers.

+[no]dnssec

Requests DNSSEC records be sent by setting the DNSSEC OK bit (DO) in the OPT record in the additional section of the query.

+[no]sigchase

Chase DNSSEC signature chains. Requires dig be compiled with -DDIG_SIGCHASE.

+trusted-key=*####*

Specifies a file containing trusted keys to be used with +sigchase. Each DNSKEY record must be on its own line.

If not specified, *dig* will look for */etc/trusted-key.key* then trusted-key.key in the current directory.

Requires dig be compiled with -DDIG_SIGCHASE.

+[no]topdown

When chasing DNSSEC signature chains perform a top-down validation. Requires dig be compiled with -DDIG_SIGCHASE.

6.1.4. Multiple Queries with dig

The BIND 9 implementation of *dig* supports specifying multiple queries on the command line (in addition to supporting the -f batch file option). Each of those queries can be supplied with its own set of flags, options and query options.

In this case, each *query* argument represent an individual query in the command-line syntax described above. Each consists of any of the standard options and flags, the name to be looked up, an optional query type and class and any query options that should be applied to that query.

A global set of query options, which should be applied to all queries, can also be supplied. These global query options must precede the first tuple of name, class, type, options, flags, and query options supplied on the command line. Any global query options (except the +[no]cmd option) can be overridden by a query-specific set of query options. For example:

```
dig +qr www.isc.org any -x 127.0.0.1 isc.org ns +noqr
```

shows how *dig* could be used from the command line to make three lookups: an ANY query for www.isc.org, a reverse lookup of 127.0.0.1 and a query for the NS records of isc.org. A global query option of *+qr* is applied, so that *dig* shows the initial query it made for each lookup. The final query has a local query option of *+noqr* which means that *dig* will not print the initial query when it looks up the NS records for isc.org.

6.1.5. IDN Support in dig

If *dig* has been built with IDN (internationalized domain name) support, it can accept and display non-ASCII domain names. *dig* appropriately converts character encoding of domain name before sending a request to DNS server or displaying a reply from the server. If you'd like to turn off the IDN support for some reason, defines the *IDN_DISABLE* environment variable. The IDN support is disabled if the variable is set when *dig* runs.

6.1.6. dig Examples

List just the top level name servers authoritative for the .de (Germany) domain:

```
$ dig de. NS +short
a.nic.de.
c.de.net.
f.nic.de.
l.de.net.
s.de.net.
z.nic.de.
```

Dig for any A or AAAA record and don't output the QUESTION section:

```
$ dig example.org any +noquestion

; <<>> DiG 9.4.1-P1 <<>> example.org any +noquestion
;; global options:  printcmd
;; Got answer:
;; ->>HEADER<<- opcode: QUERY, status: NOERROR, id: 26399
;; flags: qr rd ra; QUERY: 1, ANSWER: 3, AUTHORITY: 2, ADDITIONAL: 2

;; ANSWER SECTION:
example.org.            172317  IN      A       208.77.188.166
example.org.            21117   IN      NS      a.iana-servers.net.
example.org.            21117   IN      NS      b.iana-servers.net.

;; AUTHORITY SECTION:
example.org.            21117   IN      NS      a.iana-servers.net.
example.org.            21117   IN      NS      b.iana-servers.net.

;; ADDITIONAL SECTION:
b.iana-servers.net.     172317  IN      A       193.0.0.236
a.iana-servers.net.     172317  IN      A       192.0.34.43

;; Query time: 1 msec
;; SERVER: 127.0.0.1#53(127.0.0.1)
;; WHEN: Tue Sep  4 17:12:03 2007
;; MSG SIZE  rcvd: 153
```

Display the SOA record for the authoritative name servers for a zone:

```
# dig +nssearch example.net
SOA dns1.icann.org. hostmaster.icann.org. 2007051703 7200 3600 ⇓
  1209600 86400 from server a.iana-servers.net in 48 ms.
SOA dns1.icann.org. hostmaster.icann.org. 2007051703 7200 3600 ⇓
  1209600 86400 from server b.iana-servers.net in 132 ms.
```

6.2. host

The *host* utility emphasizes simplicity and ease of use. By default, it converts between host names and Internet addresses, but its functionality can be extended with the use of options.

```
host [-aCdlnrsTwv] [-c class] [-N ndots] [-R retries] [-t type]
```

```
[-W timeout] [-m flag] [-4] [-6] {name} [server]
```

When no arguments or options are given, *host* prints a short summary of its command line arguments and options.

name is the domain name that is to be looked up. It can also be a dotted-decimal IPv4 address or a colon-delimited IPv6 address, in which case *host* will by default perform a reverse lookup for that address. *server* is an optional argument which is either the name or IP address of the name server that *host* should query instead of the server or servers listed in */etc/resolv.conf*.

The -a (all) option is equivalent to setting the -v option and asking *host* to make a query of type ANY.

When the -C option is used, *host* will attempt to display the SOA records for zone *name* from all the listed authoritative name servers for that zone. The list of name servers is defined by the NS records that are found for the zone.

The -c option instructs to make a DNS query of class *class*. This can be used to lookup Hesiod or Chaosnet class resource records. The default class is IN (Internet).

Verbose output is generated by *host* when the -d or -v option is used. The two options are equivalent. They have been provided for backwards compatibility. In previous versions, the -d option switched on debugging traces and -v enabled verbose output.

List mode is selected by the -l option. This makes *host* perform a zone transfer for zone *name*. Transfer the zone printing out the NS, PTR and address records (A/AAAA). If combined with -a all records will be printed.

The -i option specifies that reverse lookups of IPv6 addresses should use the IP6.INT domain as defined in RFC 1886. The default is to use IP6.ARPA.

The -N option sets the number of dots that have to be in *name* for it to be considered absolute. The default value is that defined using the **ndots** statement in */etc/resolv.conf*, or 1 if no ndots statement is present. Names with fewer dots are interpreted as relative names and will be searched for in the domains listed in the search or domain directive in */etc/resolv.conf*.

The number of UDP retries for a lookup can be changed with the -R option. *number* indicates how many times *host* will repeat a query that does not get answered. The default number of retries is 1. If *number* is negative or zero, the number of retries will default to 1.

Non-recursive queries can be made via the -r option. Setting this option clears the RD – recursion desired – bit in the query which *host* makes. This should mean that the name server receiving the query will not attempt to resolve *name*. The -r option enables host to mimic the behavior of a name server by making non-recursive queries and expecting to receive answers to those queries that are usually referrals to other name servers.

By default, *host* uses UDP when making queries. The -T option makes it use a TCP connection when querying the name server. TCP will be automatically selected for queries that require it, such as zone transfer (AXFR) requests.

The -4 option forces *host* to only use IPv4 query transport. The -6 option forces **host** to only use IPv6 query transport.

The -t option is used to select the query type. *type* can be any recognized query type: CNAME, NS, SOA, SIG, KEY, AXFR, etc. When no query type is specified, *host* automatically selects an appropriate query type. By default, it looks for A records, but if the -C option was given, queries will be made for SOA records, and if *name* is a dotted-decimal IPv4 address or colon-delimited IPv6 address, *host* will query for PTR records. If a query type of IXFR is chosen the starting serial number can be specified by appending an equal followed by the starting serial number (e.g. -t IXFR=12345678).

The time to wait for a reply can be controlled through the -W and -w options. The -W option makes *host* wait for *wait* seconds. If *wait* is less than one, the wait interval is set to one second. When the -w option is used, *host* will effectively wait forever for a reply. The time to wait for a response will be set to the number of seconds given by the hardware's maximum value for an integer quantity.

The -s option tells *host* not to send the query to the next nameserver if any server responds with a SERVFAIL response, which is the reverse of normal stub resolver behavior.

The -m can be used to set the memory usage debugging flags *record*, *usage* and *trace*.

6.2.1. IDN Support in host

If *host* has been built with IDN (internationalized domain name) support, it can accept and display non-ASCII domain names. *host* appropriately converts character encoding of domain name before sending a request to DNS server or displaying a reply from the server. If you'd like to turn off the IDN support for some reason, defines the *IDN_DISABLE* environment variable. The IDN support is disabled if the variable is set when *host* runs.

6.3. nslookup

The *nslookup* command is another program to query Internet domain name servers.

nslookup has two modes: interactive and non-interactive. Interactive mode allows the user to query name servers for information about various hosts and domains or to print a list of hosts in a domain. Non-interactive mode is used to print just the name and requested information for a host or domain.

Note: Due to its arcane user interface and frequently inconsistent behavior, the use of *nslookup* is not recommended. Use *dig* instead.

6.3.1. Arguments for nslookup

```
nslookup [-option...]  [host-to-find | - [server]]
```

Interactive mode is entered in the following cases:

1. when no arguments are given (the default name server will be used);
2. when the first argument is a hyphen (-) and the second argument is the host name or Internet address of a name server.

Non-interactive mode is used when the name or Internet address of the host to be looked up is given as the first argument. The optional second argument specifies the host name or address of a name server.

Options can also be specified on the command line if they precede the arguments and are prefixed with a hyphen. For example, to change the default query type to host information, and the initial timeout to 10 seconds, type:

```
nslookup -query=hinfo -timeout=10
```

6.3.2. Interactive Commands

host [server]

Look up information for host using the current default server or using server, if specified. If *server* is an Internet address and the query type is A or PTR, the name of the host is returned. If *server* is a name and does not have a trailing period, the search list is used to qualify the name.

To look up a host not in the current domain, append a period to the name.

server *domain*

lserver *domain* Change the default server to *domain*; **lserver** uses the initial server to look up information about *domain*, while **server** uses the current default server. If an authoritative answer can't be found, the names of servers that might have the answer are returned.

root

not implemented

finger

not implemented

ls

not implemented

view

not implemented

help

not implemented

?

not implemented

exit

Exits the program.

set *keyword[=value]*

This command is used to change state information that affects the lookups. Valid keywords are:

all

Prints the current values of the frequently used options to **set**. Information about the current default server and host is also printed.

class=*value* Change the query class to one of:

IN

the Internet class

CH

the Chaos class

HS

the Hesiod class

ANY

wildcard

The class specifies the protocol group of the information.

(Default = IN; abbreviation = cl)

***[no]*debug**

Turn on or off the display of the full response packet and any intermediate response packets when searching.

(Default = nodebug; abbreviation = [no]deb)

***[no]*d2**

Turn debugging mode on or off. This displays more about what *nslookup* is doing.

(Default = nod2)

domain=*name* Sets the search list to *name*.

***[no]*search**

If the lookup request contains at least one period but doesn't end with a trailing period, append the domain names in the domain search list to the request until an answer is received.

(Default = search)

port=*value* Change the default TCP/UDP name server port to *value*.

(Default = 53; abbreviation = po)

querytype=*value*

type=*value* Change the type of the information query.

(Default = A; abbreviations = q, ty)

***[no]*recurse**

Tell the name server to query other servers if it does not have the information.

(Default = recurse; abbreviation = [no]rec)

retry=*number* Set the number of retries to number.

timeout=*number* Change the initial timeout interval for waiting for a reply to number seconds.

***[no]*vc**

Always use a virtual circuit when sending requests to the server.

(Default = novc)

***[no]*fail**

Try the next nameserver if a nameserver responds with SERVFAIL or a referral (nofail) or terminate query (fail) on such a response.

(Default = nofail)

7. Advanced DNS Features

7.1. Notify

DNS NOTIFY is a mechanism that allows master servers to notify their slave servers of changes to a zone's data. In response to a NOTIFY from a master server, the slave will check to see that its version of the zone is the current version and, if not, initiate a zone transfer.

For more information about DNS NOTIFY, see the description of the **notify** option in the section called *Boolean Options* on page 102 and the description of the zone option **also-notify** in the section called *Zone Transfers* on page 113. The NOTIFY protocol is specified in RFC 1996.

As a slave zone can also be a master to other slaves, named, by default, sends NOTIFY messages for every zone it loads. Specifying "**notify master-only;**" will cause named to only send NOTIFY for master zones that it loads.

7.2. Dynamic Update

Dynamic Update is a method for adding, replacing or deleting records in a master server by sending it a special form of DNS messages. The format and meaning of these messages is specified in RFC 2136.

Dynamic update is enabled by including an **allow-update** or **update-policy** clause in the **zone** statement. The **tkey-gssapi-credential** and **tkey-domain** clauses in the **options** statement enable the server to negotiate keys that can be matched against those in **update-policy** or **allow-update**.

Updating of secure zones (zones using DNSSEC) follows RFC 3007: RRSIG and NSEC records affected by updates are automatically regenerated by the server using an online zone key. Update authorization is based on transaction signatures and an explicit server policy.

7.3. The journal file

All changes made to a zone using dynamic update are stored in the zone's journal file. This file is automatically created by the server when the first dynamic update takes place. The name of the journal file is formed by appending the extension .jnl to the name of the corresponding zone file unless specifically overridden. The journal file is in a binary format and should not be edited manually.

The server will also occasionally write ("dump") the complete contents of the updated zone to its zone file. This is not done immediately after each dynamic update, because that would be too slow when a large zone is updated frequently. Instead, the dump is delayed by up to 15 minutes, allowing additional updates to take place.

When a server is restarted after a shutdown or crash, it will replay the journal file to incorporate into the zone any updates that took place after the last zone dump.

Changes that result from incoming incremental zone transfers are also journalled in a similar way.

The zone files of dynamic zones cannot normally be edited by hand because they are not guaranteed to contain the most recent dynamic changes – those are only in the journal file. The only way to ensure that the zone file of a dynamic zone is up to date is to run:[1]

```
rndc stop
```

If you have to make changes to a dynamic zone manually, the following procedure will work. Disable dynamic updates to the zone using:

```
rndc freeze zone
```

This will also remove the zone's .jnl file and update the master file. Edit the zone file. To reload the changed zone and re-enable dynamic updates, run:

```
rndc thaw zone
```

7.4. Incremental Zone Transfers (IXFR)

The incremental zone transfer (IXFR) protocol is a way for slave servers to transfer only changed data, instead of having to transfer the entire zone. The IXFR protocol is specified in RFC 1995, "Incremental Zone Transfer in DNS."[2]

When acting as a master, BIND 9 supports IXFR for those zones where the necessary change history information is available. These include master zones maintained by dynamic update and slave zones whose data was obtained by IXFR. For manually maintained master zones, and for slave zones obtained by performing a full zone

[1] *rndc* is covered in section 4.3.

[2] The proposed standards are listed on page 183.

transfer (AXFR), IXFR is supported only if the option **ixfr-from-differences** is set to **yes**.

When acting as a slave, BIND 9 will attempt to use IXFR unless it is explicitly disabled. For more information about disabling IXFR, see the description of the **request-ixfr** clause of the **server** statement on page 131.

7.5. Split DNS

Setting up different views, or visibility, of the DNS space to internal and external resolvers is usually referred to as a *Split DNS* setup. There are several reasons an organization would want to set up its DNS this way.

One common reason for setting up a DNS system this way is to hide "internal" DNS information from "external" clients on the Internet. There is some debate as to whether or not this is actually useful. Internal DNS information leaks out in many ways (via email headers, for example) and most savvy "attackers" can find the information they need using other means. However, since listing addresses of internal servers that external clients cannot possibly reach can result in connection delays and other annoyances, an organization may choose to use a Split DNS to present a consistent view of itself to the outside world.

Another common reason for setting up a Split DNS system is to allow internal networks that are behind filters or in RFC 1918 space (reserved IP space, as documented in RFC 1918) to resolve DNS on the Internet. Split DNS can also be used to allow mail from outside back in to the internal network.

7.5.1. Example split DNS setup

Let's say a company named *Example, Inc.* (example.com) has several corporate sites that have an internal network with reserved Internet Protocol (IP) space and an external demilitarized zone (DMZ), or "outside" section of a network, that is available to the public.

Example, Inc. wants its internal clients to be able to resolve external hostnames and to exchange mail with people on the outside. The company also wants its internal resolvers to have access to certain internal-only zones that are not available at all outside of the internal network.

In order to accomplish this, the company will set up two sets of name servers. One set will be on the inside network (in the reserved IP space) and the other set will be on bastion hosts, which are "proxy" hosts that can talk to both sides of its network, in the DMZ.

The internal servers will be configured to forward all queries, except queries for *site1.internal*, *site2.internal*, *site1.example.com*, and *site2.example.com*, to the servers in the DMZ. These internal servers will have complete sets of information for *site1.example.com*, *site2.example.com*, *site1.internal*, and *site2.internal.*

To protect the *site1.internal* and *site2.internal* domains, the internal name servers must be configured to disallow all queries to these domains from any external hosts, including the bastion hosts.

The external servers, which are on the bastion hosts, will be configured to serve the "public" version of the *site1* and *site2.example.com* zones. This could include things such as the host records for public servers (*www.example.com* and *ftp.example.com*), and mail exchange (MX) records (*a.mx.example.com* and *b.mx.example.com*).

In addition, the public *site1* and *site2.example.com* zones should have special MX records that contain wildcard ('*') records pointing to the bastion hosts. This is needed because external mail servers do not have any other way of looking up how to deliver mail to those internal hosts. With the wildcard records, the mail will be delivered to the bastion host, which can then forward it on to internal hosts.

Here's an example of a wildcard MX record:

```
*   IN MX 10 external1.example.com.
```

Now that they accept mail on behalf of anything in the internal network, the bastion hosts will need to know how to deliver mail to internal hosts. In order for this to work properly, the resolvers on the bastion hosts will need to be configured to point to the internal name servers for DNS resolution.

Queries for internal hostnames will be answered by the internal servers, and queries for external hostnames will be forwarded back out to the DNS servers on the bastion hosts.

In order for all this to work properly, internal clients will need to be configured to query *only* the internal name servers for DNS queries. This could also be enforced via selective filtering on the network.

If everything has been set properly, *Example, Inc.*'s internal clients will now be able to:

- Look up any hostnames in the *site1* and *site2.example.com* zones.
- Look up any hostnames in the *site1.internal* and *site2.internal* domains.
- Look up any hostnames on the Internet.
- Exchange mail with both internal and external people.

Hosts on the Internet will be able to:

- Look up any hostnames in the *site1* and *site2.example.com* zones.
- Exchange mail with anyone in the *site1* and *site2.example.com* zones.

Here is an example configuration for the setup just described above. Note that this is only configuration information; for information on how to configure your zone files, see the section called *Sample Configurations* (9.5) in Chapter 9.

Internal DNS server config:

```
acl internals { 172.16.72.0/24; 192.168.1.0/24; };
acl externals { bastion-ips-go-here; };
options {
    ...
    ...
    forward only;
    // forward to external servers
    forwarders {
        bastion-ips-go-here;
    };
    // sample allow-transfer (no one)
    allow-transfer { none; };
    // restrict query access
    allow-query { internals; externals; };
    // restrict recursion
    allow-recursion { internals; };
    ...
    ...
};
// sample master zone
zone "site1.example.com" {
  type master;
  file "m/site1.example.com";
  // do normal iterative resolution (do not forward)
  forwarders { };
  allow-query { internals; externals; };
  allow-transfer { internals; };
};
// sample slave zone
zone "site2.example.com" {
  type slave;
  file "s/site2.example.com";
  masters { 172.16.72.3; };
  forwarders { };
  allow-query { internals; externals; };
  allow-transfer { internals; };
};
zone "site1.internal" {
  type master;
  file "m/site1.internal";
  forwarders { };
  allow-query { internals; };
  allow-transfer { internals; }
};
```

```
zone "site2.internal" {
  type slave;
  file "s/site2.internal";
  masters { 172.16.72.3; };
  forwarders { };
  allow-query { internals };
  allow-transfer { internals; }
};
```

External (bastion host) DNS server config:

```
acl internals { 172.16.72.0/24; 192.168.1.0/24; };
acl externals { bastion-ips-go-here; };
options {
  ...
  ...
  // sample allow-transfer (no one)
  allow-transfer { none; };
  // default query access
  allow-query { any; };
  // restrict cache access
  allow-query-cache { internals; externals; };
  // restrict recursion
  allow-recursion { internals; externals; };
  ...
  ...
};
// sample slave zone
zone "site1.example.com" {
  type master;
  file "m/site1.foo.com";
    allow-transfer { internals; externals; };
};
zone "site2.example.com" {
  type slave;
  file "s/site2.foo.com";
  masters { another_bastion_host_maybe; };
   allow-transfer { internals; externals; }
};
```

In the *resolv.conf* (or equivalent) on the bastion host(s):

```
search ...
nameserver 172.16.72.2
nameserver 172.16.72.3
nameserver 172.16.72.4
```

7.6. TSIG

This is a short guide to setting up Transaction SIGnatures (TSIG) based transaction security in BIND. It describes changes to the configuration file as well as what changes are required for different features, including the process of creating transaction keys and using transaction signatures with BIND.

BIND primarily supports TSIG for server to server communication. This includes zone transfer, notify, and recursive query messages. Resolvers based on newer versions of BIND 8 have limited support for TSIG.

TSIG can also be useful for dynamic update. A primary server for a dynamic zone should control access to the dynamic update service, but IP-based access control is insufficient. The cryptographic access control provided by TSIG is far superior. The *nsupdate* program supports TSIG via the -k and -y command line options or inline by use of the key.[3]

Generate Shared Keys for Each Pair of Hosts

A shared secret is generated to be shared between *host1* and *host2*. An arbitrary key name is chosen: "host1-host2.". The key name must be the same on both hosts.[4]

Automatic Generation

The following command will generate a 128-bit (16 byte) HMAC-MD5 key as described above. Longer keys are better, but shorter keys are easier to read. Note that the maximum key length is 512 bits; keys longer than that will be digested with MD5 to produce a 128-bit key.

```
dnssec-keygen -a hmac-md5 -b 128 -n HOST host1-host2.
```

The key is in the file *Khost1-host2.+157+00000.private*. Nothing directly uses this file, but the base-64 encoded string following "Key:" can be extracted from the file and used as a shared secret:

```
Key: La/E5CjG9O+os1jq0a2jdA==
```

The string "La/E5CjG9O+os1jq0a2jdA==" can be used as the shared secret.

[3] nsupdate is covered in section 5.4.

[4] There is no particular reason for the trailing period in this key name example. It is not required. But be sure to be consistent if using it.

Manual Generation

The shared secret is simply a random sequence of bits, encoded in base-64. Most ASCII strings are valid base-64 strings (assuming the length is a multiple of 4 and only valid characters are used), so the shared secret can be manually generated.

Also, a known string can be run through *mmencode*[5] or a similar program to generate base-64 encoded data.[6] For example:

```
$ echo -n "your shared secret" | mmencode
eW91ciBzaGFyZWQgc2VjcmV0
```

Here is another example using Perl:

```
$ perl -MMIME::Base64 -e \
    'print encode_base64("your shared secret");'
eW91ciBzaGFyZWQgc2VjcmV0
```

Copying the Shared Secret to Both Machines

This is beyond the scope of DNS. A secure transport mechanism should be used. This could be secure FTP, ssh, telephone, etc.

Informing the Servers of the Key's Existence

Imagine *host1* and *host 2* are both servers. The following is added to each server's *named.conf* file:

```
key host1-host2. {
  algorithm hmac-md5;
  secret "La/E5CjG9O+os1jq0a2jdA==";
};
```

The algorithm, hmac-md5, is the only one supported by BIND. The secret is the one generated above. Since this is a secret, it is recommended that either *named.conf* be non-world readable, or the key directive be added to a non-world readable file that is included by *named.conf*.

At this point, the key is recognized. This means that if the server receives a message signed by this key, it can verify the signature. If the signature is successfully verified, the response is signed by the same key.

[5] The mmencode program is from the old Metamail package, which was one of the earliest MIME implementations.

[6] Actually, you do not need a tool to create this as long as your key is made from the allowed 64 characters, such as A-Z, a-z, 0-9, + (plus) and / (slash) (and no space).

Instructing the Server to Use the Key

Since keys are shared between two hosts only, the server must be told when keys are to be used. The following is added to the *named.conf* file for *host1*, if the IP address of *host2* is 10.1.2.3:

```
server 10.1.2.3 {
  keys { host1-host2. ;};
};
```

Multiple keys may be present, but only the first is used. This directive does not contain any secrets, so it may be in a world-readable file.

If *host1* sends a message that is a request to that address, the message will be signed with the specified key. *host1* will expect any responses to signed messages to be signed with the same key.

A similar statement must be present in *host2*'s configuration file (with *host1*'s address) for *host2* to sign request messages to *host1*.

TSIG Key Based Access Control

BIND allows IP addresses and ranges to be specified in ACL definitions and **allow-{ query | transfer | update }** directives. This has been extended to allow TSIG keys also. The above key would be denoted **key host1-host2.**

An example of an **allow-update** directive would be:

```
allow-update { key host1-host2. ;};
```

This allows dynamic updates to succeed only if the request was signed by a key named "**host1-host2.**".

You may want to read about the more powerful **update-policy** statement in the section called *Dynamic Update Policies* on page 144.

Errors

The processing of TSIG signed messages can result in several errors. If a signed message is sent to a non-TSIG aware server, a FORMERR (format error) will be returned, since the server will not understand the record. This is a result of misconfiguration, since the server must be explicitly configured to send a TSIG signed message to a specific server.

If a TSIG aware server receives a message signed by an unknown key, the response will be unsigned with the TSIG extended error code set to BADKEY. If a TSIG aware server receives a message with a signature that does not validate, the response will be unsigned with the TSIG extended error code set to BADSIG. If a TSIG aware server receives a message with a time outside of the allowed range, the response will be signed with the TSIG extended error code set to BADTIME, and the time values will be adjusted so that the response can be successfully verified. In any of these cases, the message's rcode (response code) is set to NOTAUTH (not authenticated[7]).

7.7. TKEY

TKEY is a mechanism for automatically generating a shared secret between two hosts. There are several "modes" of TKEY that specify how the key is generated or assigned. BIND 9 implements only one of these modes, the Diffie-Hellman key exchange. Both hosts are required to have a Diffie-Hellman KEY record (although this record is not required to be present in a zone). The TKEY process must use signed messages, signed either by TSIG or SIG(0). The result of TKEY is a shared secret that can be used to sign messages with TSIG. TKEY can also be used to delete shared secrets that it had previously generated.

The TKEY process is initiated by a client or server by sending a signed TKEY query (including any appropriate KEYs) to a TKEY-aware server. The server response, if it indicates success, will contain a TKEY record and any appropriate keys. After this exchange, both participants have enough information to determine the shared secret; the exact process depends on the TKEY mode. When using the Diffie-Hellman TKEY mode, Diffie-Hellman keys are exchanged, and the shared secret is derived by both participants.

7.8. SIG(0)

BIND 9 partially supports DNSSEC SIG(0) transaction signatures as specified in RFC 2535 and RFC 2931. SIG(0) uses public/private keys to authenticate messages. Access control is performed in the same manner as TSIG keys; privileges can be granted or denied based on the key name.

When a SIG(0) signed message is received, it will only be verified if the key is known and trusted by the server; the server will not attempt to locate and/or validate the key.

SIG(0) signing of multiple-message TCP streams is not supported.

The only tool shipped with BIND 9 that generates SIG(0) signed messages is *nsupdate* (introduced in section 5.4).

[7]NOTAUTH is an overloaded rcode. The correct description in this context is "not authenticated" rather than "not authoritative".

7.9. DNSSEC

Cryptographic authentication of DNS information is possible through the DNS Security (*DNSSEC-bis*) extensions, defined in RFC 4033, RFC 4034, and RFC 4035. This section describes the creation and use of DNSSEC signed zones.

In order to set up a DNSSEC secure zone, there are a series of steps which must be followed. BIND 9 ships with several tools that are used in this process, which are explained in more detail below. In all cases, the -h option prints a full list of parameters. Note that the DNSSEC tools require the keyset files to be in the working directory or the directory specified by the -d option, and that the tools shipped with BIND 9.2.x and earlier are not compatible with the current ones.

There must also be communication with the administrators of the parent and/or child zone to transmit keys. A zone's security status must be indicated by the parent zone for a DNSSEC capable resolver to trust its data. This is done through the presence or absence of a DS record at the delegation point.

For other servers to trust data in this zone, they must either be statically configured with this zone's zone key or the zone key of another zone above this one in the DNS tree.

Generating Keys

The *dnssec-keygen* program (introduced in section 5.5) is used to generate keys.

A secure zone must contain one or more zone keys. The zone keys will sign all other records in the zone, as well as the zone keys of any secure delegated zones. Zone keys must have the same name as the zone, a name type of **ZONE**, and must be usable for authentication. It is recommended that zone keys use a cryptographic algorithm designated as "mandatory to implement" by the IETF; currently the only one is RSASHA1.

The following command will generate a 768-bit RSASHA1 key for the child.example zone:

```
dnssec-keygen -a RSASHA1 -b 768 -n ZONE child.example.
```

Two output files will be produced: *Kchild.example.+005+12345.key* and *Kchild.example.+005+12345.private* (where *12345* is an example of a key tag). The key filenames contain the key name (*child.example.*), algorithm (3 is DSA, 1 is RSAMD5, 5 is RSASHA1, etc.), and the key tag (*12345* in this case). The private key (in the *.private* file) is used to generate signatures, and the public key (in the *.key* file) is used for signature verification.

To generate another key with the same properties (but with a different key tag), repeat the above command.

The public keys should be inserted into the zone file by including the *.key* files using **$INCLUDE** statements.

Signing the Zone

The *dnssec-signzone* program (introduced in section 5.6) is used to sign a zone.

Any keyset files corresponding to secure subzones should be present. The zone signer will generate NSEC and RRSIG records for the zone, as well as DS for the child zones if '-d' is specified. If '-d' is not specified, then DS RRsets for the secure child zones need to be added manually.

The following command signs the zone, assuming it is in a file called *zone.child.example*. By default, all zone keys which have an available private key are used to generate signatures.

```
dnssec-signzone -o child.example zone.child.example
```

One output file is produced: *zone.child.example.signed*. This file should be referenced by *named.conf* as the input file for the zone.

dnssec-signzone will also produce a keyset and dsset files and optionally a dlvset file. These are used to provide the parent zone administrators with the DNSKEYs (or their corresponding DS records) that are the secure entry point to the zone.

Configuring Servers

To enable named to respond appropriately to DNS requests from DNSSEC aware clients, **dnssec-enable** must be set to yes.

To enable named to validate answers from other servers both **dnssec-enable** and **dnssec-validation** must be set and some **trusted-keys** must be configured into *named.conf*.

trusted-keys are copies of DNSKEY RRs for zones that are used to form the first link in the cryptographic chain of trust. All keys listed in **trusted-keys** (and corresponding zones) are deemed to exist and only the listed keys will be used to validated the DNSKEY RRset that they are from.

trusted-keys are described in more detail later in this book. See section 10.27.

Unlike BIND 8, BIND 9 does not verify signatures on load, so zone keys for authoritative zones do not need to be specified in the configuration file.

After DNSSEC gets established, a typical DNSSEC configuration will look something like the following. It has a one or more public keys for the root. This allows answers from outside the organization to be validated. It will also have several keys for parts of the name space the organization controls. These are here to ensure that named is immune to compromises in the DNSSEC components of the security of parent zones.

```
trusted-keys {

/* Root Key */
"." 257 3 3 "BNY4wrWM1nCfJ+CXd0rVXyYmobt7sEEfK3clRbGaTwSJxrGkxJWoZu6I
            7PzJu/E9gx4UC1zGAHlXKdE4zYIpRhaBKnvcC2U9mZhkdUpd1Vso/HAd
            jNe8LmMlnzY3zy2Xy4klWOADTPzSv9eamj8V18PHGjBLaVtYvk/ln5ZA
            pjYghf+6fElrmLkdazMQ2OCnACR817DF4BBa7UR/beDHyp5iWTXWSi6X
            moJLbG9Scqc7l70KDqlvXR3M/lUUVRbkeg1IPJSidmK3ZyCllh4XSKbj
            e/45SKucHgnwU5jefMtq66gKodQj+MiA21AfUVe7u99WzTLzY3qlxDhx
            YQQ20FQ97S+LKUTpQcq27R7AT3/V5hRQxScINqwcz4jYqZD2fQdgxbcD
            TClU0CRBdiieyLMNzXG3";

/* Key for our organization's forward zone */
example.com. 257 3 5 "AwEAAaxPMcR2x0HbQV4WeZB6oEDX+r0QM65KbhTjrW1ZaAR
                     mPhEZZe3Y9ifgEuq7vZ/zGZUdEGNWy+JZzus0lUptwgjGwh
                     US1558Hb4JKUbbOTcM8pwXlj0EiX3oDFVmjHO444gLkBOUK
                     Uf/mC7HvfwYH/Be22GnClrinKJp1Og4ywzO9WglMk7jbfW3
                     3gUKvirTHr25GL7STQUzBb5Usxt8lgnyTUHs1t3JwCY5hKZ
                     6CqFxmAVZP20igTixin/1LcrgX/KMEGd/biuvF4qJCyduie
                     HukuY3H4XMAcR+xia2 nIUPvm/oyWR8BW/hWdzOvnSCThlH
                     f3xiYleDbt/o1OTQ09A0=";


/* Key for our reverse zone. */
2.0.192.IN-ADDRPA.NET. 257 3 5 "AQOnS4xn/IgOUpBPJ3bogzwcxOdNax071L18Q
                               qZnQQQAVVr+iLhGTnNGp3HoWQLUIzKrJVZ3zg
                               gy3WwNT6kZo6c0tszYqbtvchmgQC8CzKojM/W
                               16i6MG/ea fGU3siaOdS0yOI6BgPsw+YZdzlY
                               MaIJGf4M4dyoKIhzdZyQ2bYQrjyQ4LB0lC7aO
                               nsMyYKHHYeRv PxjIQXmdqgOJGq+vsevG06zW
                               +1xgYJh9rCIfnmlGX/KMgxLPG2vXTD/RnLX+D
                               3T3UL7HJYHJhAZD5L59VvjSPsZJHeDCUyWYrv
                               PZesZDIRvhDD52SKvbheeTJUm6EhkzytNN2SN
                               96QRk8j/iI8ib";
};

options {
        ...
        dnssec-enable yes;
        dnssec-validation yes;
};
```

Note: None of the keys listed in this example are valid. In particular, the root key is not valid.

7.10. IPv6 Support in BIND 9

BIND 9 fully supports all currently defined forms of IPv6 name to address and address to name lookups. It will also use IPv6 addresses to make queries when running on an IPv6 capable system.

For forward lookups, BIND 9 supports only AAAA records. RFC 3363 deprecated the use of A6 records, and client-side support for A6 records was accordingly removed from BIND 9. However, authoritative BIND 9 name servers still load zone files containing A6 records correctly, answer queries for A6 records, and accept zone transfer for a zone containing A6 records.

For IPv6 reverse lookups, BIND 9 supports the traditional "nibble" format used in the *ip6.arpa* domain, as well as the older, deprecated *ip6.int* domain. Older versions of BIND 9 supported the "binary label" (also known as "bitstring") format, but support of binary labels has been completely removed per RFC 3363. Many applications in BIND 9 do not understand the binary label format at all any more, and will return an error if given. In particular, an authoritative BIND 9 name server will not load a zone file containing binary labels.

Format and Structure of IPv6 addresses (AAAA)

IPv6 addresses are 128-bit identifiers for interfaces and sets of interfaces which were introduced in the DNS to facilitate scalable Internet routing. There are three types of addresses: *Unicast*, an identifier for a single interface; *Anycast*, an identifier for a set of interfaces; and *Multicast*, an identifier for a set of interfaces. Here the global Unicast address scheme is described. For more information, see RFC 3587, "IPv6 Global Unicast Address Format."

IPv6 unicast addresses consist of a global routing prefix, a subnet identifier, and an interface identifier.

The global routing prefix is provided by the upstream provider or ISP, and (roughly) corresponds to the IPv4 network section of the address range. The subnet identifier is for local subnetting, much the same as subnetting an IPv4 /16 network into /24 subnets. The interface identifier is the address of an individual interface on a given network; in IPv6, addresses belong to interfaces rather than to machines.

The subnetting capability of IPv6 is much more flexible than that of IPv4: subnetting can be carried out on bit boundaries, in much the same way as Classless InterDomain Routing (CIDR), and the DNS PTR representation ("nibble" format) makes setting up reverse zones easier.

The Interface Identifier must be unique on the local link, and is usually generated automatically by the IPv6 implementation, although it is usually possible to override the default setting if necessary. A typical IPv6 address might look like:

```
2001:db8:201:9:a00:20ff:fe81:2b32
```

IPv6 address specifications often contain long strings of zeros, so the architects have included a shorthand for specifying them. The double colon ('::') indicates the longest possible string of zeros that can fit, and can be used only once in an address.

Address Lookups Using AAAA Records

The IPv6 AAAA record is a parallel to the IPv4 A record, and, unlike the deprecated A6 record, specifies the entire IPv6 address in a single record. For example,

```
$ORIGIN example.com.
host            3600    IN      AAAA    2001:db8::1
```

Use of IPv4-in-IPv6 mapped addresses is not recommended. If a host has an IPv4 address, use an A record, not a AAAA, with ::ffff:192.168.42.1 as the address.

Address to Name Lookups Using Nibble Format

When looking up an address in nibble format, the address components are simply reversed, just as in IPv4, and ip6.arpa. is appended to the resulting name. For example, the following would provide reverse name lookup for a host with address 2001:db8::1.

```
$ORIGIN 0.0.0.0.0.0.0.0.8.b.d.0.1.0.0.2.ip6.arpa.
1.0.0.0.0.0.0.0.0.0.0.0.0.0.0.0    14400 IN   PTR  host.example.com.
```

8. The BIND 9 Lightweight Resolver

8.1. The Lightweight Resolver Library

Traditionally applications have been linked with a stub resolver library that sends recursive DNS queries to a local caching name server.

IPv6 once introduced new complexity into the resolution process, such as following A6 chains and DNAME records, and simultaneous lookup of IPv4 and IPv6 addresses. Though most of the complexity was then removed, these are hard or impossible to implement in a traditional stub resolver.

BIND 9 therefore can also provide resolution services to local clients using a combination of a lightweight resolver library and a resolver daemon process running on the local host. These communicate using a simple UDP-based protocol, the "lightweight resolver protocol" that is distinct from and simpler than the full DNS protocol.

8.2. Running a Resolver Daemon

To use the lightweight resolver interface, the system must run the resolver daemon *lwresd* or a local name server configured with a **lwres** statement.

By default, applications using the lightweight resolver library will make UDP requests to the IPv4 loopback address (127.0.0.1) on port 921. The address can be overridden by **lwserver** lines in */etc/resolv.conf*.

The daemon currently only looks in the DNS, but in the future it may use other sources such as */etc/hosts*, NIS, etc.

The *lwresd* daemon is essentially a caching-only name server that responds to requests using the lightweight resolver protocol rather than the DNS protocol. Because it needs to run on each host, it is designed to require no or minimal configuration. Unless configured otherwise, it uses the name servers listed on **nameserver** lines in */etc/resolv.conf* as forwarders, but is also capable of doing the resolution autonomously if none are specified.

The *lwresd* daemon may also be configured with a named.conf style configuration file, in */etc/lwresd.conf* by default. A name server may also be configured to act as a lightweight resolver daemon using the **lwres** statement in *named.conf*.[1]

[1]This is covered in section 10.6.

8.3. Using lwresd

The *lwresd* program is the daemon providing name lookup services to clients that use the BIND 9 lightweight resolver library. It is essentially a stripped-down, caching-only name server that answers queries using the BIND 9 lightweight resolver protocol rather than the DNS protocol. (The *lwresd* program is a link to the *named* executable and is like running *named* with the -l switch.)

lwresd listens for resolver queries on a UDP port on the IPv4 loopback interface, 127.0.0.1. This means that *lwresd* can only be used by processes running on the local machine. By default UDP port number 921 is used for lightweight resolver requests and responses.

Incoming lightweight resolver requests are decoded by the server which then resolves them using the DNS protocol. When the DNS lookup completes, *lwresd* encodes the answers in the lightweight resolver format and returns them to the client that made the request.

If */etc/resolv.conf* contains any nameserver entries, *lwresd* sends recursive DNS queries to those servers. This is similar to the use of forwarders in a caching name server. If no nameserver entries are present, or if forwarding fails, *lwresd* resolves the queries autonomously starting at the root name servers, using a built-in list of root server hints.

8.3.1. Options for lwresd

```
lwresd [-c config-file] [-C config-file] [-d debug-level] [-f]
   [-g] [-i pid-file] [-m flag] [-n #cpus] [-P port] [-p port]
   [-s] [-t directory] [-u user] [-v]
```

-4

Use IPv4 only even if the host machine is capable of IPv6. -4 and -6 are mutually exclusive.

-6

Use IPv6 only even if the host machine is capable of IPv4. -4 and -6 are mutually exclusive.

-c *config-file*

Use *config-file* as the configuration file instead of the default, */etc/lwresd.conf*. -c can not be used with -C.

-C *config-file*

Use *config-file* as the configuration file instead of the default, */etc/resolv.conf*. -C can not be used with -c.

-d *debug-level*

Set the daemon's debug level to *debug-level*. Debugging traces from *lwresd* become more verbose as the debug level increases.

-f

Run the server in the foreground (i.e. do not daemonize).

-g

Run the server in the foreground and force all logging to stderr.

-i *pid-file*

Use *pid-file* as the PID file instead of the default, */var/run/lwresd.pid*.

-m *flag*

Turn on memory usage debugging flags. Possible flags are usage, trace, record, size, and mctx. These correspond to the ISC_MEM_DEBUG*XXXX* flags described in <*isc/mem.h*>.

-n *#cpus*

Create *#cpus* worker threads to take advantage of multiple CPUs. If not specified, *lwresd* will try to determine the number of CPUs present and create one thread per CPU. If it is unable to determine the number of CPUs, a single worker thread will be created.

-P *port*

Listen for lightweight resolver queries on port *port*. If not specified, the default is port 921.

-p *port*

Send DNS lookups to port *port*. If not specified, the default is port 53. This provides a way of testing the lightweight resolver daemon with a name server that listens for queries on a non-standard port number.

-s

Write memory usage statistics to stdout on exit.

Note: This option is mainly of interest to BIND 9 developers and may be removed or changed in a future release.

-t *directory*

Chroot to *directory* after processing the command line arguments, but before reading the configuration file.

Warning: This option should be used in conjunction with the -u option, as chrooting a process running as root doesn't enhance security on most systems; the way chroot(2) is defined allows a process with root privileges to escape a chroot jail.

-u *user* Setuid to *user* after completing privileged operations, such as creating sockets that listen on privileged ports.

-v

Report the version number and exit.

9. Name Server Configuration

In this chapter, some suggested configurations along with guidelines for their use are provided. Reasonable values for certain option settings are suggested. This chapter also introduces the configuration file elements, comments, and address match lists.

BIND 9 configuration is broadly similar to BIND 8; however, there are a few new areas of configuration, such as views. BIND 8 configuration files should work with few alterations in BIND 9, although more complex configurations should be reviewed to check if they can be more efficiently implemented using the new features found in BIND 9.

BIND 4 configuration files can be converted to the new format using the shell script *contrib/named-bootconf/named-bootconf.sh.*[1]

9.1. Configuration File Elements

Following is a list of elements used throughout the BIND configuration file documentation:

acl_name The name of an *address_match_list* as defined by the acl statement.

address_match_list A list of one or more *ip_addr*, *ip_prefix*, *key_id*, or *acl_name* elements. For details, see section 9.2.

masters_list A named list of one or more *ip_addr* with optional *key_id* and/or *ip_port*. A *masters_list* may include other *masters_lists*.

domain_name A quoted string which will be used as a DNS name, for example "my.test.domain".

dotted_decimal One to four integers valued 0 through 255 separated by dots ('.'), such as 123, 45.67 or 89.123.45.67.

ip4_addr An IPv4 address with exactly four elements in *dotted_decimal* notation.

ip6_addr An IPv6 address, such as 2001:db8::1234. IPv6 scoped addresses that have ambiguity on their scope zones must be disambiguated by an appropriate zone ID with the percent character ('%') as delimiter. It is strongly recommended

[1]The *named-bootconf* tool is installed on some operating systems with their custom installation of BIND.

to use string zone names rather than numeric identifiers, in order to be robust against system configuration changes. However, since there is no standard mapping for such names and identifier values, currently only interface names as link identifiers are supported, assuming one-to-one mapping between interfaces and links. For example, a link-local address fe80::1 on the link attached to the interface *ne0* can be specified as fe80::1%ne0. Note that on most systems link-local addresses always have the ambiguity, and need to be disambiguated.

ip_addr An *ip4_addr* or *ip6_addr*.

ip_port An IP port number. The number is limited to 0 through 65535, with values below 1024 typically restricted to use by processes running as root. In some cases, an asterisk ('*') character can be used as a placeholder to select a random high-numbered port.

ip_prefix An IP network specified as an *ip_addr*, followed by a slash ('/') and then the number of bits in the netmask. Trailing zeros in a *ip_addr* may omitted. For example, 127/8 is the network 127.0.0.0 with netmask 255.0.0.0 and 1.2.3.0/28 is network 1.2.3.0 with netmask 255.255.255.240.

When specifying a prefix involving a IPv6 scoped address the scope may be omitted. In that case the prefix will match packets from any scope.

key_id A *domain_name* representing the name of a shared key, to be used for transaction security.

key_list A list of one or more *key_ids*, separated by semicolons and ending with a semicolon.

number A non-negative 32-bit integer (i.e., a number between 0 and 4294967295, inclusive). Its acceptable value might further be limited by the context in which it is used.

path_name A quoted string which will be used as a pathname, such as zones/master/my.test.domain.

size_spec A number, the word **unlimited**, or the word **default**. An **unlimited** *size_spec* requests unlimited use, or the maximum available amount. A **default** *size_spec* uses the limit that was in force when the server was started. A number can optionally be followed by a scaling factor: **K** or **k** for kilobytes, **M** or **m** for megabytes, and **G** or **g** for gigabytes, which scale by 1024, 1024*1024, and 1024*1024*1024 respectively. The value must be representable as a 64-bit unsigned integer (0 to 18446744073709551615, inclusive). Using **unlimited** is the best way to safely set a really large number.

yes_or_no Either **yes** or **no**. The words **true** and **false** are also accepted, as are the numbers **1** and **0**.

dialup_option One of **yes**, **no**, **notify**, **notify-passive**, **refresh** or **passive**. When used in a zone, **notify-passive**, **refresh**, and **passive** are restricted to slave and stub zones. (See section 10.8.1 for details.)

9.2. Address Match Lists

Syntax

```
address_match_list = address_match_list_element ;
  [ address_match_list_element; ... ]
address_match_list_element = [ ! ] (ip_address [/length] |
   key key_id | acl_name | { address_match_list } )
```

Definition and Usage

Address match lists are primarily used to determine access control for various server operations. They are also used in the **listen-on** and **sortlist** statements. The elements which constitute an address match list can be any of the following:

- an IP address (IPv4 or IPv6)
- an IP prefix (in '/' notation)
- a key ID, as defined by the **key** statement
- the name of an address match list defined with the **acl** statement
- a nested address match list enclosed in braces

Elements can be negated with a leading exclamation mark ('!'), and the match list names "**any**", "**none**", "**localhost**", and "**localnets**" are predefined. More information on those names can be found in the description of the **acl** statement in section 10.1.

The addition of the **key** clause made the name of this syntactic element something of a misnomer, since security keys can be used to validate access without regard to a host or network address. Nonetheless, the term "address match list" is still used throughout the documentation.

When a given IP address or prefix is compared to an address match list, the list is traversed in order until an element matches. The interpretation of a match depends on whether the list is being used for access control, defining listen-on ports, or in a sortlist, and whether the element was negated.

When used as an access control list, a non-negated match allows access and a negated match denies access. If there is no match, access is denied. The clauses **allow-notify**,

allow-recursion, **allow-query**, **allow-query-on**, **allow-query-cache**, **allow-query-cache-on**, **allow-transfer**, **allow-update**, **allow-update-forwarding**, and **blackhole** all use address match lists. Similarly, the listen-on option will cause the server to not accept queries on any of the machine's addresses which do not match the list.

Because of the first-match aspect of the algorithm, an element that defines a subset of another element in the list should come before the broader element, regardless of whether either is negated. For example, in **1.2.3/24; ! 1.2.3.13;** the 1.2.3.13 element is completely useless because the algorithm will match any lookup for 1.2.3.13 to the 1.2.3/24 element. Using **! 1.2.3.13; 1.2.3/24** fixes that problem by having 1.2.3.13 blocked by the negation but all other 1.2.3.* hosts fall through.

9.3. Comment Syntax

The BIND 9 comment syntax allows for comments to appear anywhere that whitespace may appear in a BIND configuration file. To appeal to programmers of all kinds, they can be written in the C, C++, or shell/perl style.

Syntax

```
/* This is a BIND comment as in C */
// This is a BIND comment as in C++
# This is a BIND comment as in common UNIX shells and perl
```

Definition and Usage

Comments may appear anywhere that whitespace may appear in a BIND configuration file.

C-style comments start with the two characters /* (slash, star) and end with */ (star, slash). Because they are completely delimited with these characters, they can be used to comment only a portion of a line or to span multiple lines.

C-style comments cannot be nested. For example, the following is not valid because the entire comment ends with the first */:

```
/* This is the start of a comment.
   This is still part of the comment.
/* This is an incorrect attempt at nesting a comment. */
   This is no longer in any comment. */
```

C++-style comments start with the two characters // (slash, slash) and continue to the end of the physical line. They cannot be continued across multiple physical lines; to have one logical comment span multiple lines, each line must use the // pair.

For example:

```
// This is the start of a comment.  The next line
// is a new comment, even though it is logically
// part of the previous comment.
```

Shell-style (or perl-style, if you prefer) comments start with the character # (number sign) and continue to the end of the physical line, as in C++ comments.

For example:

```
# This is the start of a comment.  The next line
# is a new comment, even though it is logically
# part of the previous comment.
```

Warning: You cannot use the semicolon (';') character to start a comment such as you would in a zone file. The semicolon indicates the end of a configuration statement.

9.4. Configuration File Grammar

A BIND 9 configuration consists of statements and comments. Statements end with a semicolon. Statements and comments are the only elements that can appear without enclosing braces. Many statements contain a block of sub-statements, which are also terminated with a semicolon.

The following statements are supported:

acl defines a named IP address matching list, for access control and other uses.

controls declares control channels to be used by the *rndc* utility.

include includes a file.

key specifies key information for use in authentication and authorization using TSIG.

logging specifies what the server logs, and where the log messages are sent.

lwres configures named to also act as a lightweight resolver daemon (*lwresd*).

masters defines a named masters list for inclusion in stub and slave zone masters clauses.

options controls global server configuration options and sets defaults for other statements.

server sets certain configuration options on a per-server basis.

trusted-keys defines trusted DNSSEC keys.

view defines a view.

zone defines a zone.

The **logging** and **options** statements may only occur once per configuration.

The many configurations are covered in chapter 10.

9.5. Sample Configurations

A Caching-only Name Server

The following sample configuration[2] is appropriate for a caching-only name server for use by clients internal to a corporation. All queries from outside clients are refused using the **allow-query** option. Alternatively, the same effect could be achieved using suitable firewall rules.

```
// Two corporate subnets we wish to allow queries from.
acl corpnets { 192.168.4.0/24; 192.168.7.0/24; };
options {
     // Working directory
     directory "/etc/namedb";
     // Do not allow access to cache
     allow-query-cache { none; };
     allow-query { corpnets; };
};
// Provide a reverse mapping for the
// loopback address 127.0.0.1
zone "0.0.127.in-addr.arpa" {
     type master;
     file "localhost.rev";
     notify no;
};
```

An Authoritative-only Name Server

This sample configuration is for an authoritative-only server that is the master server for "*example.com*" and a slave for the subdomain "*eng.example.com*".

```
options {
     // Working directory
```

[2] The **allow-query-cache** option was added in BIND 9.4. For details, see page 110.

```
     directory "/etc/namedb";
     // This is the default
     allow-query { any; };
     // Do not provide recursive service
     recursion no;
};
// Provide a reverse mapping for the loopback
// address 127.0.0.1
zone "0.0.127.in-addr.arpa" {
     type master;
     file "localhost.rev";
     notify no;
};
// We are the master server for example.com
zone "example.com" {
     type master;
     file "example.com.db";
     // IP addresses of slave servers allowed to
     // transfer example.com
     allow-transfer {
          192.168.4.14;
          192.168.5.53;
     };
};
// We are a slave server for eng.example.com
zone "eng.example.com" {
     type slave;
     file "eng.example.com.bk";
     // IP address of eng.example.com master server
     masters { 192.168.4.12; };
};
```

10. BIND 9 Configuration Reference

10.1. acl Statement

acl Statement Grammar

```
acl acl-name {
    address_match_list
};
```

acl Statement Definition and Usage

The **acl** statement assigns a symbolic name to an address match list. It gets its name from a primary use of address match lists: Access Control Lists (ACLs).

Note that an address match list's name must be defined with **acl** before it can be used elsewhere; no forward references are allowed.

The following ACLs are built-in:

any Matches all hosts.

none Matches no hosts.

localhost Matches the IPv4 and IPv6 addresses of all network interfaces on the system.

localnets Matches any host on an IPv4 or IPv6 network for which the system has an interface. Some systems do not provide a way to determine the prefix lengths of local IPv6 addresses. In such a case, **localnets** only matches the local IPv6 addresses, just like **localhost**.

10.2. controls Statement

controls Statement Grammar

```
controls {
   [ inet ( ip_addr | * ) [ port ip_port ]
```

```
      allow { address_match_list }
                keys { key_list }; ]
   [ inet ...; ]
   [ unix path perm number owner number group number ⇓
     keys { key_list }; ]
};
```

controls Statement Definition and Usage

The **controls** statement declares control channels to be used by system administrators to control the operation of the name server. These control channels are used by the *rndc* utility to send commands to and retrieve non-DNS results from a name server. (*rndc* is covered in section 4.3.)

An **inet** control channel is a TCP socket listening at the specified *ip_port* on the specified *ip_addr*, which can be an IPv4 or IPv6 address. An *ip_addr* of "*" (asterisk) is interpreted as the IPv4 wildcard address; connections will be accepted on any of the system's IPv4 addresses. To listen on the IPv6 wildcard address, use an *ip_addr* of ::. If you will only use *rndc* on the local host, using the loopback address (127.0.0.1 or ::1) is recommended for maximum security.

If no port is specified, port 953 is used. The asterisk "*" cannot be used for *ip_port*.

The ability to issue commands over the control channel is restricted by the **allow** and **keys** clauses. Connections to the control channel are permitted based on the *address_match_list*. This is for simple IP address based filtering only; any *key_id* elements of the *address_match_list* are ignored.

A **unix** control channel is a UNIX domain socket listening at the specified path in the file system. Access to the socket is specified by the **perm**, **owner** and **group** clauses. Note on some platforms (SunOS and Solaris) the permissions (**perm**) are applied to the parent directory as the permissions on the socket itself are ignored. This UNIX domain controls support was added in BIND 9.4.

The primary authorization mechanism of the command channel is the key_list, which contains a list of *key_id*'s. Each *key_id* in the *key_list* is authorized to execute commands over the control channel. See chapter 4 for information about configuring keys in *rndc*.

If no **controls** statement is present, *named* will set up a default control channel listening on the loopback address 127.0.0.1 and its IPv6 counterpart ::1. In this case, and also when the **controls** statement is present but does not have a **keys** clause, *named* will attempt to load the command channel key from the file *rndc.key* in /etc (or whatever sysconfdir[1] was specified as when BIND was built). To create a *rndc.key* file, run:[2]

```
rndc-confgen -a
```

[1] See page 10 for details about sysconfdir.

[2] *rndc-confgen* is covered in section 23.

The *rndc.key* feature was created to ease the transition of systems from BIND 8, which did not have digital signatures on its command channel messages and thus did not have a **keys** clause. It makes it possible to use an existing BIND 8 configuration file in BIND 9 unchanged, and still have *rndc* work the same way *ndc* worked in BIND 8, simply by executing the command **rndc-confgen -a** after BIND 9 is installed.

Since the *rndc.key* feature is only intended to allow the backward-compatible usage of BIND 8 configuration files, this feature does not have a high degree of configurability. You cannot easily change the key name or the size of the secret, so you should make a *rndc.conf* with your own key if you wish to change those things. The *rndc.key* file also has its permissions set such that only the owner of the file (the user that *named* is running as) can access it. If you desire greater flexibility in allowing other users to access *rndc* commands, then you need to create a *rndc.conf* file and make it group readable by a group that contains the users who should have access.

To disable the command channel, use an empty **controls** statement:

```
controls { };
```

10.3. include Statement

include Statement Grammar

```
include filename;
```

include Statement Definition and Usage

The **include** statement inserts the specified file at the point where the **include** statement is encountered. The **include** statement facilitates the administration of configuration files by permitting the reading or writing of some things but not others. For example, the statement could include private keys that are readable only by the name server.

10.4. key Statement

key Statement Grammar

```
key key_id {
    algorithm string;
    secret string;
};
```

key Statement Definition and Usage

The **key** statement defines a shared secret key for use with TSIG (see section 7.6) or the command channel (see section 10.2).

The **key** statement can occur at the top level of the configuration file or inside a **view** statement. Keys defined in top-level **key** statements can be used in all views. Keys intended for use in a **controls** statement must be defined at the top level.

The *key_id*, also known as the key name, is a domain name uniquely identifying the key. It can be used in a **server** statement to cause requests sent to that server to be signed with this key, or in address match lists to verify that incoming requests have been signed with a key matching this name, algorithm, and secret.

The *algorithm_id* is a string that specifies a security/authentication algorithm. Named supports hmac-md5, hmac-sha1, hmac-sha224, hmac-sha256, hmac-sha384 and hmac-sha512 TSIG authentication. Truncated hashes are supported by appending the minimum number of required bits preceded by a dash, e.g. hmac-sha1-80. The *secret_string* is the secret to be used by the algorithm, and is treated as a base-64 encoded string.

10.5. logging Statement

logging Statement Grammar

```
logging {
   [ channel channel_name {
     ( file path name
         [ versions ( number | unlimited ) ]
         [ size size spec ]
       | syslog syslog_facility
       | stderr
       | null );
     [ severity (critical | error | warning | notice |
                 info | debug [ level ] | dynamic ); ]
     [ print-category yes or no; ]
     [ print-severity yes or no; ]
     [ print-time yes or no; ]
   }; ]
   [ category category_name {
    channel_name ; [ channel_name ; ... ]
   }; ]
...
};
```

logging Statement Definition and Usage

The **logging** statement configures a wide variety of logging options for the name server. Its **channel** phrase associates output methods, format options and severity levels with a name that can then be used with the **category** phrase to select how various classes of messages are logged.

Only one **logging** statement is used to define as many channels and categories as are wanted. If there is no **logging** statement, the logging configuration will be:

```
logging {
     category default { default_syslog; default_debug; };
     category unmatched { null; };
};
```

In BIND 9, the logging configuration is only established when the entire configuration file has been parsed. In BIND 8, it was established as soon as the **logging** statement was parsed. When the server is starting up, all logging messages regarding syntax errors in the configuration file go to the default channels, or to standard error if the "-g" option was specified.

The channel Phrase

All log output goes to one or more *channels*; you can make as many of them as you want.

Every channeldefinition must include a destination clause that says whether messages selected for the channel go to a file, to a particular syslog facility, to the standard error stream, or are discarded. It can optionally also limit the message severity level that will be accepted by the channel (the default is **info**), and whether to include a *named*-generated time stamp, the category name and/or severity level (the default is not to include any).

The **null** destination clause causes all messages sent to the channel to be discarded; in that case, other options for the channel are meaningless.

The **file** destination clause directs the channel to a disk file. It can include limitations both on how large the file is allowed to become, and how many versions of the file will be saved each time the file is opened.

If you use the **versions** log file option, then *named* will retain that many backup versions of the file by renaming them when opening. For example, if you choose to keep three old versions of the file *lamers.log*, then just before it is opened *lamers.log.1* is renamed to *lamers.log.2*, *lamers.log.0* is renamed to *lamers.log.1*, and *lamers.log* is renamed to *lamers.log.0*. You can say **versions unlimited** to not limit the number of versions. If a **size** option is associated with the log file, then renaming is only done when the file being opened exceeds the indicated size. No backup versions are kept by default; any existing log file is simply appended.

The **size** option for files is used to limit log growth. If the file ever exceeds the size, then *named* will stop writing to the file unless it has a **versions** option associated with it. If backup versions are kept, the files are rolled as described above and a new one begun. If there is no **versions** option, no more data will be written to the log until some out-of-band mechanism removes or truncates the log to less than the maximum size. The default behavior is not to limit the size of the file.

Example usage of the **size** and **versions** options:

```
channel an_example_channel {
    file "example.log" versions 3 size 20m;
    print-time yes;
    print-category yes;
};
```

The **syslog** destination clause directs the channel to the system log. Its argument is a syslog facility as described in the *syslog* man page. Known facilities are **kern**, **user**, **mail**, **daemon**, **auth**, **syslog**, **lpr**, **news**, **uucp**, **cron**, **authpriv**, **ftp**, **local0**, **local1**, **local2**, **local3**, **local4**, **local5**, **local6** and **local7**, however not all facilities are supported on all operating systems. How **syslog** will handle messages sent to this facility is described in the *syslog.conf* man page. If you have a system which uses a very old version of syslog that only uses two arguments to the openlog() function, then this clause is silently ignored.

The **severity** clause works like **syslog**'s "priorities", except that they can also be used if you are writing straight to a file rather than using **syslog**. Messages which are not at least of the severity level given will not be selected for the channel; messages of higher severity levels will be accepted.

If you are using **syslog**, then the *syslog.conf* priorities will also determine what eventually passes through. For example, defining a channel facility and severity as **daemon** and **debug** but only logging **daemon.warning** via *syslog.conf* will cause messages of severity **info** and **notice** to be dropped. If the situation were reversed, with *named* writing messages of only **warning** or higher, then *syslogd* would print all messages it received from the channel.

The **stderr** destination clause directs the channel to the server's standard error stream. This is intended for use when the server is running as a foreground process, for example when debugging a configuration.

The server can supply extensive debugging information when it is in debugging mode. If the server's global debug level is greater than zero, then debugging mode will be active. The global debug level is set either by starting the *named* server with the -d flag followed by a positive integer, or by running:[3]

[3] *rndc* is covered in section 4.3.

```
rndc trace
```

The global debug level can be set to zero, and debugging mode turned off, by running:

```
rndc notrace
```

All debugging messages in the server have a debug level, and higher debug levels give more detailed output. Channels that specify a specific debug severity, for example:

```
channel specific_debug_level {
    file "foo";
    severity debug 3;
};
```

will get debugging output of level 3 or less any time the server is in debugging mode, regardless of the global debugging level. Channels with **dynamic** severity use the server's global debug level to determine what messages to print.

If **print-time** has been turned on, then the date and time will be logged. **print-time** may be specified for a **syslog** channel, but is usually pointless since *syslog* also logs the date and time. If **print-category** is requested, then the category of the message will be logged as well. Finally, if **print-severity** is on, then the severity level of the message will be logged. The **print-** options may be used in any combination, and will always be printed in the following order: time, category, severity. Here is an example where all three **print-** options are on:

```
28-Feb-2000 15:05:32.863 general: notice: running
```

There are four predefined channels that are used for *named*'s default logging as follows. How they are used is described in the section called *The **category** Phrase* on page 90.

```
channel default_syslog {
    // send to syslog's daemon facility
    syslog daemon;
    // only send priority info and higher
    severity info;
};

channel default_debug {
    // write to named.run in the working directory
    // Note: stderr is used instead of "named.run"
    // if the server is started with the '-f' option.
    file "named.run";
    // log at the server's current debug level
```

```
    severity dynamic;
};

channel default_stderr {
    // writes to stderr
    stderr;
    // only send priority info and higher
    severity info;
};

channel null {
   // toss anything sent to this channel
   null;
};
```

The **default_debug** channel has the special property that it only produces output when the server's debug level is nonzero. It normally writes to a file called "*named.run*" in the server's working directory.

For security reasons, when the "-u" command line option is used, the "*named.run*" file is created only after *named* has changed to the new UID, and any debug output generated while *named* is starting up and still running as root is discarded. If you need to capture this output, you must run the server with the "-g" option and redirect standard error to a file.

Once a channel is defined, it cannot be redefined. Thus you cannot alter the built-in channels directly, but you can modify the default logging by pointing categories at channels you have defined.

The category Phrase

There are many categories, so you can send the logs you want to see wherever you want, without seeing logs you don't want. If you don't specify a list of channels for a category, then log messages in that category will be sent to the **default** category instead. If you don't specify a default category, the following "default default" is used:

```
category default { default_syslog; default_debug; };
```

As an example, let's say you want to log security events to a file, but you also want keep the default logging behavior. You'd specify the following:

```
channel my_security_channel {
    file "my_security_file";
    severity info;
};
```

```
category security {
    my_security_channel;
    default_syslog;
    default_debug;
};
```

To discard all messages in a category, specify the **null** channel:

```
category xfer-out { null; };
category notify { null; };
```

Following are the available categories and brief descriptions of the types of log information they contain. More categories may be added in future BIND releases.

default The default category defines the logging options for those categories where no specific configuration has been defined.

general The catch-all. Many things still aren't classified into categories, and they all end up here.

database Messages relating to the databases used internally by the name server to store zone and cache data.

security Approval and denial of requests.

config Configuration file parsing and processing.

resolver DNS resolution, such as the recursive lookups performed on behalf of clients by a caching name server.

xfer-in Zone transfers the server is receiving.

xfer-out Zone transfers the server is sending.

notify The NOTIFY protocol.

client Processing of client requests.

unmatched Messages that named was unable to determine the class of or for which there was no matching view. A one line summary is also logged to the client category. This category is best sent to a file or stderr, by default it is sent to the null channel.

network Network operations.

update Dynamic updates.

update-security Approval and denial of update requests.

queries Specify where queries should be logged to. At startup, specifying the category queries will also enable query logging unless **querylog** option has been specified. The query log entry reports the client's IP address and port number, and the query name, class and type. It also reports whether the Recursion Desired flag was set (+ if set, - if not set), if the query was signed (S), EDNS was in use (E), if DO (DNSSSEC ok) was set (D), or if CD (checking disabled) was set (C).

```
client 127.0.0.1#62536:  query:  www.example.com IN AAAA +SE
client ::1#62537:  query:  www.example.net IN AAAA -SE
```

dispatch Dispatching of incoming packets to the server modules where they are to be processed.

dnssec DNSSEC and TSIG protocol processing.

lame-servers Lame servers. These are misconfigurations in remote servers, discovered by BIND 9 when trying to query those servers during resolution.

delegation-only Delegation only. Logs queries that have have been forced to NXDOMAIN as the result of a delegation-only zone or a delegation-only in a hint or stub zone declaration.

edns-disabled Log queries that have been forced to use plain DNS due to timeouts. This is often due to the remote servers not being RFC 1034 compliant – not always returning FORMERR (format error) or similar to EDNS queries and other extensions to the DNS when they are not understood. In other words, this is targeted at servers that fail to respond to DNS queries that they don't understand. This **edns-disabled** logging category was added in BIND 9.5.

Note: the log message can also be due to packet loss. Before reporting servers for non-RFC 1034 compliance they should be re-tested to determine the nature of the non-compliance. This testing should prevent or reduce the number of false-positive reports.

Note: eventually *named* will have to stop treating such timeouts as due to RFC 1034 non compliance and start treating it as plain packet loss as falsely classifying packet loss. Falsely classifying packet loss as due to RFC 1034 non compliance impacts on DNSSEC validation which requires EDNS for the DNSSEC records to be returned.

10.6. lwres Statement

lwres Statement Grammar

This is the grammar of the **lwres** statement in the named.conf file:

```
lwres {
    [ listen-on { ip_addr [port ip_port] ;
      [ ip_addr [port ip_port] ; ... ] }; ]
    [ view view_name; ]
    [ search { domain_name ; [ domain_name ; ... ] }; ]
    [ ndots number; ]
};
```

lwres Statement Definition and Usage

The **lwres** statement configures the name server to also act as a lightweight resolver server. (See the section 8.2 about *Running a Resolver Daemon* in Chapter 8.) There may be multiple **lwres** statements configuring lightweight resolver servers with different properties.

The **listen-on** statement specifies a list of addresses (and ports) that this instance of a lightweight resolver daemon should accept requests on. If no port is specified, port 921 is used. If this statement is omitted, requests will be accepted on 127.0.0.1, port 921.

The **view** statement binds this instance of a lightweight resolver daemon to a view in the DNS name space, so that the response will be constructed in the same manner as a normal DNS query matching this view. If this statement is omitted, the default view is used, and if there is no default view, an error is triggered.

The **search** statement is equivalent to the **search** statement in */etc/resolv.conf*. It provides a list of domains which are appended to relative names in queries.

The **ndots** statement is equivalent to the **ndots** statement in */etc/resolv.conf*. It indicates the minimum number of dots in a relative domain name that should result in an exact match lookup before search path elements are appended.

10.7. masters Statement

masters Statement Grammar

```
masters name [ port ip_port ] {
  ( masters_list | ip_addr [port ip_port] [key key] ) ;
  [...] };
```

masters Statement Definition and Usage

masters lists allow for a common set of masters to be easily used by multiple stub and slave zones.

10.8. options Statement

options Statement Grammar

This is the grammar of the **options** statement in the named.conf file:

```
options {
    [ version version_string; ]
    [ hostname hostname_string; ]
    [ server-id server_id_string; ]
    [ directory path_name; ]
    [ key-directory path_name; ]
    [ named-xfer path_name; ]
    [ tkey-gssapi-credential principal; ]
    [ tkey-domain domainname; ]
    [ tkey-dhkey key_name key_tag; ]
    [ cache-file path_name; ]
    [ dump-file path_name; ]
    [ memstatistics-file path_name; ]
    [ pid-file path_name; ]
    [ recursing-file path_name; ]
    [ statistics-file path_name; ]
    [ stats-server [ address ip4_addr ] port ip_port ; ]
    [ stats-server-v6 ... ; ]
    [ zone-statistics yes_or_no; ]
    [ auth-nxdomain yes_or_no; ]
    [ deallocate-on-exit yes_or_no; ]
    [ dialup dialup_option; ]
    [ fake-iquery yes_or_no; ]
    [ fetch-glue yes_or_no; ]
    [ flush-zones-on-shutdown yes_or_no; ]
    [ has-old-clients yes_or_no; ]
    [ host-statistics yes_or_no; ]
    [ host-statistics-max number; ]
    [ minimal-responses yes_or_no; ]
    [ multiple-cnames yes_or_no; ]
    [ notify yes_or_no | explicit | master-only; ]
    [ recursion yes_or_no; ]
    [ rfc2308-type1 yes_or_no; ]
    [ use-id-pool yes_or_no; ]
    [ maintain-ixfr-base yes_or_no; ]
    [ dnssec-enable yes_or_no; ]
    [ dnssec-validation yes_or_no; ]
    [ dnssec-lookaside domain trust-anchor domain; ]
    [ dnssec-must-be-secure domain yes_or_no; ]
```

```
[ dnssec-accept-expired yes_or_no; ]
[ forward ( only | first ); ]
[ forwarders {
  [ ip_addr [port  ip_port] ; ... ] }; ]
[ dual-stack-servers [port ip_port] {
    ( domain_name [port ip_port] |
      ip_addr [port ip_port] ) ;
    ... }; ]
[ check-names ( master | slave | response )
    ( warn | fail | ignore ); ]
[ check-mx ( warn | fail | ignore ); ]
[ check-wildcard yes_or_no; ]
[ check-integrity yes_or_no; ]
[ check-mx-cname ( warn | fail | ignore ); ]
[ check-srv-cname ( warn | fail | ignore ); ]
[ check-sibling yes_or_no; ]
[ allow-notify { address_match_list }; ]
[ allow-query { address_match_list }; ]
[ allow-query-on { address_match_list }; ]
[ allow-query-cache { address_match_list }; ]
[ allow-query-cache-on { address_match_list }; ]
[ allow-transfer { address_match_list }; ]
[ allow-recursion { address_match_list }; ]
[ allow-recursion-on { address_match_list }; ]
[ allow-update { address_match_list }; ]
[ allow-update-forwarding {
   address_match_list }; ]
[ update-check-ksk yes_or_no; ]
[ allow-v6-synthesis { address_match_list }; ]
[ blackhole { address_match_list }; ]
[ avoid-v4-udp-ports { port_list }; ]
[ avoid-v6-udp-ports { port_list }; ]
[ listen-on [ port ip_port ] {
   address_match_list }; ]
[ listen-on-v6 [ port ip_port ] {
   address_match_list }; ]
[ query-source ( ( ip4_addr | * )
    [ port ( ip_port | * ) ] |
    [ address ( ip4_addr | * ) ]
    [ port ( ip_port | * ) ] ) ; ]
[ query-source-v6 ( ( ip6_addr | * )
    [ port ( ip_port | * ) ] |
    [ address ( ip6_addr | * ) ]
    [ port ( ip_port | ) ] ) ; ]
[ use-queryport-pool yes_or_no; ]
```

```
[ queryport-pool-ports number; ]
[ queryport-pool-interval number; ]
[ max-transfer-time-in number; ]
[ max-transfer-time-out number; ]
[ max-transfer-idle-in number; ]
[ max-transfer-idle-out number; ]
[ tcp-clients number; ]
[ recursive-clients number; ]
[ serial-query-rate number; ]
[ serial-queries number; ]
[ tcp-listen-queue number; ]
[ transfer-format
   ( one-answer | many-answers ); ]
[ transfers-in  number; ]
[ transfers-out number; ]
[ transfers-per-ns number; ]
[ transfer-source
  (ip4_addr | *) [port ip_port] ; ]
[ transfer-source-v6
  (ip6_addr | *) [port ip_port] ; ]
[ alt-transfer-source
  (ip4_addr | *) [port ip_port] ; ]
[ alt-transfer-source-v6
  (ip6_addr | *) [port ip_port] ; ]
[ use-alt-transfer-source yes_or_no; ]
[ notify-delay seconds ; ]
[ notify-source (ip4_addr | *) [port ip_port] ; ]
[ notify-source-v6 (ip6_addr | *) [port ip_port] ; ]
[ also-notify { ip_addr [port ip_port] ;
  [ ip_addr [port ip_port] ; ... ] }; ]
[ max-ixfr-log-size number; ]
[ max-journal-size size_spec; ]
[ coresize size_spec ; ]
[ datasize size_spec ; ]
[ files size_spec ; ]
[ stacksize size_spec ; ]
[ cleaning-interval number; ]
[ heartbeat-interval number; ]
[ interface-interval number; ]
[ statistics-interval number; ]
[ topology { address_match_list }];
[ sortlist { address_match_list }];
[ rrset-order { order_spec ;
  [ order_spec ; ... ] ] };
[ lame-ttl number; ]
```

```
    [ max-ncache-ttl number; ]
    [ max-cache-ttl number; ]
    [ sig-validity-interval number ; ]
    [ min-roots number; ]
    [ use-ixfr yes_or_no ; ]
    [ provide-ixfr yes_or_no; ]
    [ request-ixfr yes_or_no; ]
    [ treat-cr-as-space yes_or_no ; ]
    [ min-refresh-time number ; ]
    [ max-refresh-time number ; ]
    [ min-retry-time number ; ]
    [ max-retry-time number ; ]
    [ port ip_port; ]
    [ additional-from-auth yes_or_no ; ]
    [ additional-from-cache yes_or_no ; ]
    [ random-device path_name ; ]
    [ max-cache-size size_spec ; ]
    [ match-mapped-addresses yes_or_no; ]
    [ preferred-glue ( A | AAAA / NONE ); ]
    [ edns-udp-size number; ]
    [ max-udp-size number; ]
    [ root-delegation-only [ exclude { namelist } ] ; ]
    [ querylog yes_or_no ; ]
    [ disable-algorithms domain {
      algorithm; [ algorithm; ] }; ]
    [ acache-enable yes_or_no ; ]
    [ acache-cleaning-interval number; ]
    [ max-acache-size size_spec ; ]
    [ clients-per-query number ; ]
    [ max-clients-per-query number ; ]
    [ masterfile-format ( text | raw ) ; ]
    [ empty-server name ; ]
    [ empty-contact name ; ]
    [ empty-zones-enable yes_or_no ; ]
    [ disable-empty-zone zone_name ; ]
    [ zero-no-soa-ttl yes_or_no ;
]
    [ zero-no-soa-ttl-cache yes_or_no ; ]
};
```

options Statement Definition and Usage

The **options** statement sets up global options to be used by BIND. This statement may appear only once in a configuration file. If there is no **options** statement, an **options** block with each option set to its default will be used.

directory

The working directory of the server. Any non-absolute pathnames in the configuration file will be taken as relative to this directory. The default location for most server output files (e.g. *named.run*) is this directory. If a directory is not specified, the working directory defaults to '.', the directory from which the server was started. The directory specified should be an absolute path.

key-directory

When performing dynamic update of secure zones, the directory where the public and private key files should be found, if different than the current working directory. The directory specified must be an absolute path.

named-xfer

This option is obsolete. It was used in BIND 8 to specify the pathname to the *named-xfer* program. In BIND 9, no separate *named-xfer* program is needed; its functionality is built into the name server.

tkey-gssapi-credential

The security credential with which the server should authenticate keys requested by the GSS-TSIG protocol. Currently only Kerberos 5 authentication is available and the credential is a Kerberos principal which the server can acquire through the default system key file, normally */etc/krb5.keytab*. Normally this principal is of the form "dns/server.domain". To use GSS-TSIG, **tkey-domain** must also be set.

tkey-domain

The domain appended to the names of all shared keys generated with **TKEY**. When a client requests a **TKEY** exchange, it may or may not specify the desired name for the key. If present, the name of the shared key will be "client specified part" + "tkey-domain". Otherwise, the name of the shared key will be "random hex digits" + "tkey-domain". In most cases, the **domainname** should be the server's domain name, or an otherwise non-existent subdomain like "_tkey.*domainname*". If you are using GSS-TSIG, this variable must be defined .

tkey-dhkey

The Diffie-Hellman key used by the server to generate shared keys with clients using the Diffie-Hellman mode of **TKEY**. The server must be able to load the public and private keys from files in the working directory. In most cases, the keyname should be the server's host name.

cache-file

This is for testing only. Do not use.

dump-file

The pathname of the file the server dumps the database to when instructed to do so with:[4]

```
rndc dumpdb
```

If not specified, the default is *named_dump.db*.

memstatistics-file

The pathname of the file the server writes memory usage statistics to on exit. Must be specified to be enabled. The commonly used filename is *named.memstats*.

pid-file

The pathname of the file the server writes its process ID in. If not specified, the default is */var/run/named.pid*. The *pid-file* is used by programs that want to send signals to the running name server. Specifying **pid-file none** disables the use of a PID file – no file will be written and any existing one will be removed. Note that **none** is a keyword, not a filename, and therefore is not enclosed in double quotes.

recursing-file

The pathname of the file the server dumps the queries that are currently recursing when instructed to do so with:

```
rndc recursing
```

If not specified, the default is *named.recursing*.

statistics-file

The pathname of the file the server appends statistics to when instructed to do so using:

```
rndc stats
```

If not specified, the default is *named.stats* in the server's current directory. The format of the file is described in the section called *The Statistics File* on page 127.

stats-server

The IPv4 **address** and/or **port** number to run the HTTP server on for providing statistics in XML format via XML. For example:

```
stats-server address 127.0.0.1 port 8080;
```

Or:

[4] *rndc* is introduced in section 4.3.

```
// XML stats on http-alt port and all 0.0.0.0 interfaces
stats-server port 8080;
```

Note: This feature is considered experimental and the syntax and usage may change.

The **stats-server** capability is only available when BIND *named* is built with libxml support. (This is not available in the standard *named*; see page 10 for details.) When built with libxml support and configured with **stats-server**, *named* can serve the statistics in XML with a simple XSL stylesheet via an embedded HTTP server. **stats-server** was introduced in BIND 9.5.

Some web browsers, like Firefox, can render the XML. (The statistics are not sent in HTML.) There are plans for software to be written for automated monitoring and realtime display of stats. The XML includes: server uptime and boot time, UDP in/out socket statistics, memory usage, views, zone status, list of tasks and threads, and minimal query statistics.

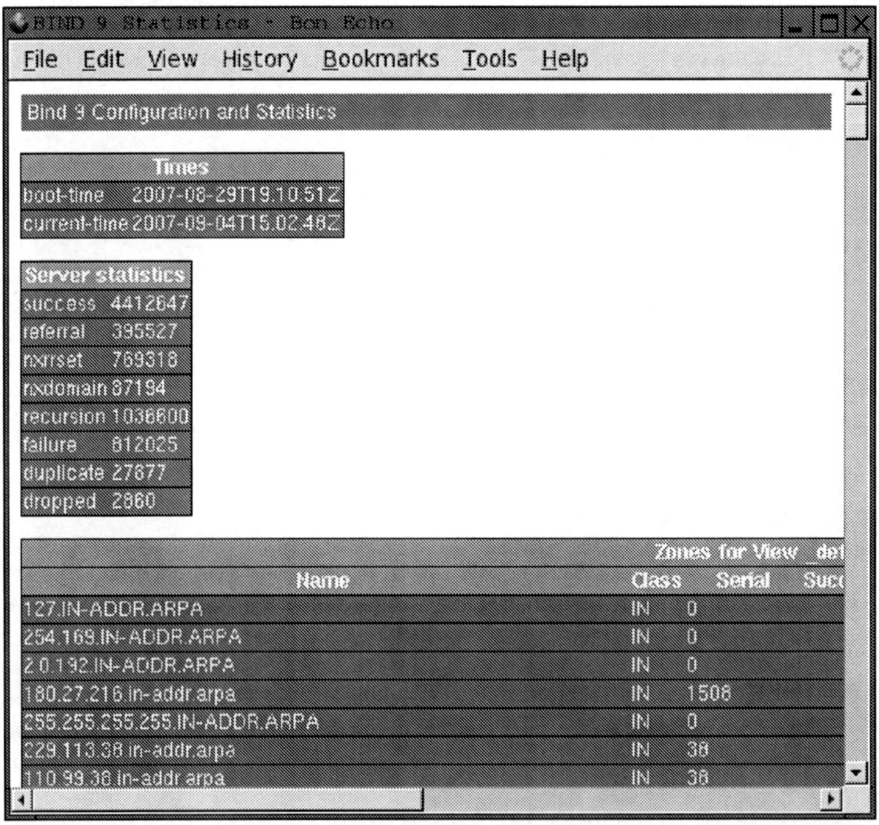

stats-server-v6

This is not implemented yet. See **stats-server** above.

port

The UDP/TCP port number the server uses for receiving and sending DNS protocol traffic. The default is 53. This option is mainly intended for server testing; a server using a port other than 53 will not be able to communicate with the global DNS.

random-device

The source of entropy to be used by the server. Entropy is primarily needed for DNSSEC operations, such as TKEY transactions and dynamic update of signed zones. This options specifies the device (or file) from which to read entropy. If this is a file, operations requiring entropy will fail when the file has been exhausted. If not specified, the default value is */dev/random* (or equivalent) when present, and none otherwise. The **random-device** option takes effect during the initial configuration load at server startup time and is ignored on subsequent reloads.

preferred-glue

If specified, the listed type (A or AAAA) will be emitted before other glue in the additional section of a query response. The default is not to prefer any type (NONE).

root-delegation-only

Turn on enforcement of delegation-only in TLDs (top level domains) and root zones with an optional exclude list.

Note some TLDs are not delegation only (e.g. “DE”, “LV”, “US” and “MUSEUM”).

```
options {
 root-delegation-only exclude {
    "de"; "lv"; "us"; "museum"; };
};
```

disable-algorithms

Disable the specified DNSSEC algorithms at and below the specified name. Multiple **disable-algorithms** statements are allowed. Only the most specific will be applied.

dnssec-lookaside

When set, **dnssec-lookaside** provides the validator with an alternate method to validate DNSKEY records at the top of a zone. When a DNSKEY is at or below a domain specified by the deepest **dnssec-lookaside**, and the normal dnssec validation has left the key untrusted, the **trust-anchor** will be append to the key name and a DLV (DNSSEC Lookaside Validation) record will be looked up to see if it can validate the key. If the DLV record validates a DNSKEY (similarly to the way a DS record does), the DNSKEY RRset is deemed to be trusted.

dnssec-must-be-secure

Specify hierarchies which must be or may not be secure (signed and validated). If **yes**, then named will only accept answers if they are secure. If **no**, then normal dnssec validation applies allowing for insecure answers to be accepted. The specified domain must be under a **trusted-key** or **dnssec-lookaside** must be active.

10.8.1. Boolean Options

auth-nxdomain

If **yes**, then the **AA** bit is always set on NXDOMAIN (no-such-domain) responses, even if the server is not actually authoritative. The default is **no**; this is a change from BIND 8. If you are using very old DNS software, you may need to set it to **yes**.

deallocate-on-exit

This option was used in BIND 8 to enable checking for memory leaks on exit. BIND 9 ignores the option and always performs the checks.

dialup

If **yes**, then the server treats all zones as if they are doing zone transfers across a dial-on-demand dialup link, which can be brought up by traffic originating from this server. This has different effects according to zone type and concentrates the zone maintenance so that it all happens in a short interval, once every **heartbeat-interval** and hopefully during the one call. It also suppresses some of the normal zone maintenance traffic. The default is **no**.

The **dialup** option may also be specified in the **view** and **zone** statements, in which case it overrides the global **dialup** option.

If the zone is a master zone, then the server will send out a NOTIFY request to all the slaves (default). This should trigger the zone serial number check in the slave (providing it supports NOTIFY) allowing the slave to verify the zone while the connection is active. The set of servers to which NOTIFY is sent can be controlled by **notify** and **also-notify**.

If the zone is a slave or stub zone, then the server will suppress the regular "zone up to date" (refresh) queries and only perform them when the **heartbeat-interval** expires in addition to sending NOTIFY requests.

Finer control can be achieved by using **notify** which only sends NOTIFY messages, **notify-passive** which sends NOTIFY messages and suppresses the normal refresh queries, **refresh** which suppresses normal refresh processing and sends refresh queries when the **heartbeat-interval** expires, and **passive** which just disables normal refresh processing.

dialup mode	normal refresh	heart-beat refresh	heart-beat notify
no (default)	yes	no	no
yes	no	yes	yes
notify	yes	no	yes
refresh	no	yes	no
passive	no	no	no
notify-passive	no	no	yes

Note that normal NOTIFY processing is not affected by **dialup**.

fake-iquery

In BIND 8, this option enabled simulating the obsolete DNS query type IQUERY. BIND 9 never does IQUERY simulation.

fetch-glue

This option is obsolete. In BIND 8, **fetch-glue yes** caused the server to attempt to fetch glue resource records it didn't have when constructing the additional data section of a response. This is now considered a bad idea and BIND 9 never does it.

flush-zones-on-shutdown

When the nameserver exits due receiving SIGTERM, flush or do not flush any pending zone writes. The default is **flush-zones-on-shutdown no**.

has-old-clients

This option was incorrectly implemented in BIND 8, and is ignored by BIND 9. To achieve the intended effect of **has-old-clients yes**, specify the two separate options **auth-nxdomain yes** and **rfc2308-type1 no** instead.

host-statistics

In BIND 8, this enables keeping of statistics for every host that the name server interacts with. Not implemented in BIND 9.

maintain-ixfr-base

This option is obsolete. It was used in BIND 8 to determine whether a transaction log was kept for Incremental Zone Transfer. BIND 9 maintains a transaction log whenever possible. If you need to disable outgoing incremental zone transfers, use **provide-ixfr no**.

minimal-responses

If **yes**, then when generating responses the server will only add records to the authority and additional data sections when they are required (e.g. delegations, negative responses). This may improve the performance of the server. The default is **no**.

multiple-cnames

This option was used in BIND 8 to allow a domain name to have multiple CNAME records in violation of the DNS standards. BIND 9.2 onwards always strictly enforces the CNAME rules both in master files and dynamic updates.

notify

If **yes** (the default), DNS NOTIFY messages are sent when a zone the server is authoritative for changes. (For details, see the section called *Notify* on page 55.) The messages are sent to the servers listed in the zone's NS records (except the master server identified in the SOA MNAME field), and to any servers listed in the **also-notify** option.

If **master-only**, notifies are only sent for master zones.[5] If **explicit**, notifies are sent only to servers explicitly listed using **also-notify**. If **no**, no notifies are sent.

The **notify** option may also be specified in the **zone** statement, in which case it overrides the **options notify** statement. It would only be necessary to turn off this option if it caused slaves to crash.

recursion

If **yes**, and a DNS query requests recursion, then the server will attempt to do all the work required to answer the query. If recursion is off and the server does not already know the answer, it will return a referral response. The default is **yes**. Note that setting **recursion no** does not prevent clients from getting data from the server's cache; it only prevents new data from being cached as an effect of client queries. Caching may still occur as an effect the server's internal operation, such as NOTIFY address lookups. See also **fetch-glue** above on page 103 and **allow-recursion** ACL on page 110.

rfc2308-type1

Setting this to **yes** will cause the server to send NS records along with the SOA record for negative answers. The default is **no**.

Note: Not yet implemented in BIND 9.

use-id-pool

This option is obsolete. BIND 9 always allocates query IDs from a pool.

zone-statistics

If **yes**, the server will collect statistical data on all zones (unless specifically turned off on a per-zone basis by specifying **zone-statistics no** in the **zone** statement). These statistics may be accessed using **rndc stats**, which will dump them to the file listed in the **statistics-file**. See also the section called *The Statistics File* on page 127.

[5]The **master-only** notify type was added in BIND 9.4.

use-ixfr

This option is obsolete. If you need to disable IXFR to a particular server or servers, see the information on the **provide-ixfr** option on page 130. Also see *Incremental Zone Transfers (IXFR)* in section 7.4.

provide-ixfr

See the description of **provide-ixfr** in the section called ***server*** *Statement Definition and Usage* on page 130.

request-ixfr

See the description of **request-ixfr** in the section called ***server*** *Statement Definition and Usage* on page 131.

treat-cr-as-space

This option was used in BIND 8 to make the server treat carriage return ("**\r**") characters the same way as a space or tab character, to facilitate loading of zone files on a UNIX system that were generated on an NT or DOS machine. In BIND 9, both UNIX "**\n**" and NT/DOS "**\r\n**" newlines are always accepted, and the option is ignored.

additional-from-auth, additional-from-cache

These options control the behavior of an authoritative server when answering queries which have additional data, or when following CNAME and DNAME chains.

When both of these options are set to **yes** (the default) and a query is being answered from authoritative data (a zone configured into the server), the additional data section of the reply will be filled in using data from other authoritative zones and from the cache. In some situations this is undesirable, such as when there is concern over the correctness of the cache, or in servers where slave zones may be added and modified by untrusted third parties. Also, avoiding the search for this additional data will speed up server operations at the possible expense of additional queries to resolve what would otherwise be provided in the additional section.

For example, if a query asks for an MX record for host *foo.example.com*, and the record found is "MX 10 mail.example.net", normally the address records (A and AAAA) for *mail.example.net* will be provided as well, if known, even though they are not in the *example.com* zone. Setting these options to **no** disables this behavior and makes the server only search for additional data in the zone it answers from.

These options are intended for use in authoritative-only servers, or in authoritative-only views. Attempts to set them to **no** without also specifying **recursion no** will cause the server to ignore the options and log a warning message.

Specifying **additional-from-cache no** actually disables the use of the cache not only for additional data lookups but also when looking up the answer. This is usually the desired behavior in an authoritative-only server where the correctness of the cached data is an issue.

When a name server is non-recursively queried for a name that is not below the apex of any served zone, it normally answers with an "upwards referral" to the root servers or the servers of some other known parent of the query name. Since the data in an upwards referral comes from the cache, the server will not be able to provide upwards referrals when **additional-from-cache no** has been specified. Instead, it will respond to such queries with REFUSED. This should not cause any problems since upwards referrals are not required for the resolution process.

match-mapped-addresses

If **yes**, then an IPv4-mapped IPv6 address will match any address match list entries that match the corresponding IPv4 address. Enabling this option is sometimes useful on IPv6-enabled Linux systems, to work around a kernel quirk that causes IPv4 TCP connections such as zone transfers to be accepted on an IPv6 socket using mapped addresses, causing address match lists designed for IPv4 to fail to match. The use of this option for any other purpose is discouraged.

ixfr-from-differences

When **yes** and the server loads a new version of a master zone from its zone file or receives a new version of a slave file by a non-incremental zone transfer, it will compare the new version to the previous one and calculate a set of differences. The differences are then logged in the zone's journal file such that the changes can be transmitted to downstream slaves as an incremental zone transfer.

By allowing incremental zone transfers to be used for non-dynamic zones, this option saves bandwidth at the expense of increased CPU and memory consumption at the master. In particular, if the new version of a zone is completely different from the previous one, the set of differences will be of a size comparable to the combined size of the old and new zone version, and the server will need to temporarily allocate memory to hold this complete difference set.

ixfr-from-differences also accepts **master** and **slave** at the view and options levels which causes **ixfr-from-differences** to apply to all master or slave zones respectively.[6]

multi-master

This should be set when you have multiple masters for a zone and the addresses refer to different machines. If **yes**, *named* will not log when the serial number on the master is less than what *named* currently has. The default is **no**.

dnssec-enable

Enable DNSSEC support in *named*. Unless set to **yes**, *named* behaves as if it does not support DNSSEC. The default is **yes**. (The default was **no** previous to BIND 9.4.)

[6]This master and slaves addition for **ixfr-from-differences** was added in BIND 9.4.

dnssec-validation

Enable DNSSEC validation in *named*. Note **dnssec-enable** also needs to be set to **yes** to be effective. The default is **no**. This option was added in BIND 9.4.

dnssec-accept-expired

Accept expired signatures when verifying DNSSEC signatures. The default is **no**. Setting this option to "**yes**" leaves *named* vulnerable to replay attacks. This feature was added in BIND 9.4.

querylog

Specify whether query logging should be started when *named* starts. If **querylog** is not specified, then the query logging is determined by the presence of the logging category **queries**.

check-names

This option is used to restrict the character set and syntax of certain domain names in master files and/or DNS responses received from the network. The default varies according to usage area. For **master** zones the default is **fail**. For **slave** zones the default is **warn**. For answers received from the network (**response**) the default is **ignore**.

The rules for legal hostnames and mail domains are derived from RFC 952 and RFC 821 as modified by RFC 1123.

check-names applies to the owner names of A, AAA and MX records. It also applies to the domain names in the RDATA of NS, SOA and MX records. It also applies to the RDATA of PTR records where the owner name indicated that it is a reverse lookup of a hostname (the owner name ends in IN-ADDR.ARPA, IP6.ARPA, or IP6.INT).

check-mx

Check whether the MX record appears to refer to a IP address. The default is to **warn**. Other possible values are **fail** and **ignore**.

check-wildcard

This option is used to check for non-terminal wildcards. The use of non-terminal wildcards is almost always as a result of a failure to understand the wildcard matching algorithm (RFC 1034). This option affects master zones. The default (**yes**) is to check for non-terminal wildcards and issue a warning. This was added in BIND 9.4.

check-integrity

Perform post load zone integrity checks on master zones. This checks that MX and SRV records refer to address (A or AAAA) records and that glue address records exist for delegated zones. For MX and SRV records only in-zone hostnames are checked (for out-of-zone hostnames use *named-checkzone)*. For

NS records only names below top of zone are checked (for out-of-zone names and glue consistency checks use *named-checkzone*). The default is **yes**. This was added in BIND 9.4.

check-mx-cname

If **check-integrity** is set then fail, warn or ignore MX records that refer to CNAMES. The default is to **warn**. This was added in BIND 9.4.

check-srv-cname

If **check-integrity** is set then fail, warn or ignore SRV records that refer to CNAMES. The default is to **warn**. This was added in BIND 9.4.

check-sibling

When performing integrity checks, also check that sibling glue exists. The default is **yes**. This was added in BIND 9.4.

zero-no-soa-ttl

When returning authoritative negative responses to SOA queries set the TTL of the SOA recored returned in the authority section to zero. The default is **yes**. This option was added in BIND 9.4.

zero-no-soa-ttl-cache

When caching a negative response to a SOA query set the TTL to zero. The default is **no**. This option was added in BIND 9.4.

update-check-ksk

When regenerating the RRSIGs following a UPDATE request to a secure zone, check the KSK flag on the DNSKEY RR to determine if this key should be used to generate the RRSIG. This flag is ignored if there are not DNSKEY RRs both with and without a KSK. The default is **yes**. This zone option was added in BIND 9.4.

try-tcp-refresh

Try to refresh the zone using TCP if UDP queries fail. For BIND 8 compatibility, the default is **yes**. This option was added in BIND 9.5.

10.9. Forwarding

The forwarding facility can be used to create a large site-wide cache on a few servers, reducing traffic over links to external name servers. It can also be used to allow queries by servers that do not have direct access to the Internet, but wish to look up exterior names anyway. Forwarding occurs only on those queries for which the server is not authoritative and does not have the answer in its cache.

forward

This option is only meaningful if the **forwarders** list is not empty. A value of first, the default, causes the server to query the forwarders first – and if that doesn't answer the question, the server will then look for the answer itself. If only is specified, the server will only query the forwarders.

forwarders

Specifies the IP addresses to be used for forwarding. The default is the empty list (no forwarding).

Forwarding can also be configured on a per-domain basis, allowing for the global forwarding options to be overridden in a variety of ways. You can set particular domains to use different forwarders, or have a different **forward only/first** behavior, or not forward at all. (For details, see page 139.)

10.10. Dual-stack Servers

Dual-stack servers are used as servers of last resort to work around problems in reachability due the lack of support for either IPv4 or IPv6 on the host machine.

dual-stack-servers

Specifies host names or addresses of machines with access to both IPv4 and IPv6 transports. If a hostname is used, the server must be able to resolve the name using only the transport it has. If the machine is dual stacked, then the **dual-stack-servers** have no effect unless access to a transport has been disabled on the command line (e.g. **named -4**).

10.11. Access Control

Access to the server can be restricted based on the IP address of the requesting system. See the section called *Address Match Lists* on page 77 for details on how to specify IP address lists.

allow-notify

Specifies which hosts are allowed to notify this server, a slave, of zone changes in addition to the zone masters. **allow-notify** may also be specified in the **zone** statement, in which case it overrides the **options allow-notify** statement. It is only meaningful for a slave zone. If not specified, the default is to process notify messages only from a zone's master.

allow-query

Specifies which hosts are allowed to ask ordinary DNS questions. **allow-query** may also be specified in the **zone** statement, in which case it overrides the **options allow-query** statement. If not specified, the default is to allow queries from all hosts.

Note: **allow-query-cache** is now used to specify access to the cache. Since BIND 9.4.1, if **allow-query**, **allow-recursion**, and **allow-query-cache** aren't defined, then queries will only be available from **localnets** and the **localhost**. (This is different than the previous default allow behavior.)

allow-query-on

Specifies which local addresses can accept ordinary DNS questions. This makes it possible, for instance, to allow queries on internal-facing interfaces but disallow them on external-facing ones, without necessarily knowing the internal network's addresses. This option was added in BIND 9.5.

allow-query-on may also be specified in the **zone** statement, in which case it overrides the **options allow-query-on** statement.

If not specified, the default is to allow queries on all addresses.

Note: **allow-query-cache** is used to specify access to the cache.

allow-query-cache

Specifies which hosts are allowed to get answers from the cache. If **allow-query-cache** is not set then **allow-recursion** is used if set, otherwise **allow-query** is used if set, otherwise the default (**localnets**; **localhost**;) is used.

This option was added in BIND 9.4. (The usage changed from version 9.4 to 9.4.1; the original behavior did not cross-inherit with **allow-recursion**.) Earlier versions used **allow-query** to set query access to the cache.

allow-query-cache-on

Specifies which local addresses can give answers from the cache. If not specified, the default is to allow cache queries on any address, **localnets** and **localhost**. This option was added in BIND 9.5.

allow-recursion

Specifies which hosts are allowed to make recursive queries through this server.[7] If **allow-recursion** is not set, then **allow-query-cache** is used if set; otherwise **allow-query** is used if set; otherwise the default (**localnets; localhost;**) is used. (In versions earlier than BIND 9.4.1, if not specified, it did not inherit values and the default was to allow recursive queries from the builtin acls **localnets** and **localhost**.)

[7] Also see the recursion option on page 104.

allow-recursion-on

Specifies which local addresses can accept recursive queries. If not specified, the default is to allow recursive queries on all addresses. This option was added in BIND 9.5.

allow-update

Specifies which hosts are allowed to submit Dynamic DNS updates for master zones. The default is to deny updates from all hosts. Note that allowing updates based on the requestor's IP address is insecure; see section 7.2 on page 55 for details.

allow-update-forwarding

Specifies which hosts are allowed to submit Dynamic DNS updates to slave zones to be forwarded to the master. The default is **{ none; }**, which means that no update forwarding will be performed. To enable update forwarding, specify **allow-update-forwarding { any; };**. Specifying values other than **{ none; }** or **{ any; }** is usually counterproductive, since the responsibility for update access control should rest with the master server, not the slaves.

Note that enabling the update forwarding feature on a slave server may expose master servers relying on insecure IP address based access control to attacks; see *Dynamic Update Security* in section 12.7 for more details.

allow-v6-synthesis

This option was introduced for the smooth transition from AAAA to A6 and from "nibble labels" to binary labels. However, since both A6 and binary labels were then deprecated, this option was also deprecated. It is now ignored with some warning messages.

allow-transfer

Specifies which hosts are allowed to receive zone transfers from the server. **allow-transfer** may also be specified in the **zone** statement, in which case it overrides the **options allow-transfer** statement. If not specified, the default is to allow transfers to all hosts.

blackhole

Specifies a list of addresses that the server will not accept queries from or use to resolve a query. Queries from these addresses will not be responded to. The default is **none**.

10.12. Interfaces

The interfaces and ports that the server will answer queries from may be specified using the **listen-on** option. **listen-on** takes an optional port and an *address_match_list*.

The server will listen on all interfaces allowed by the address match list. If a port is not specified, port 53 will be used.

Multiple **listen-on** statements are allowed. For example,

```
listen-on { 5.6.7.8; };
listen-on port 1234 { !1.2.3.4; 1.2/16; };
```

will enable the name server on port 53 for the IP address 5.6.7.8, and on port 1234 of an address on the machine in net 1.2 that is not 1.2.3.4.

If no **listen-on** is specified, the server will listen on port 53 on all interfaces.

The **listen-on-v6** option is used to specify the interfaces and the ports on which the server will listen for incoming queries sent using IPv6.

When

```
{ any; }
```

is specified as the *address_match_list* for the **listen-on-v6** option, the server does not bind a separate socket to each IPv6 interface address as it does for IPv4 if the operating system has enough API support for IPv6 (specifically if it conforms to RFC 3493 and RFC 3542). Instead, it listens on the IPv6 wildcard address. If the system only has incomplete API support for IPv6, however, the behavior is the same as that for IPv4.

A list of particular IPv6 addresses can also be specified, in which case the server listens on a separate socket for each specified address, regardless of whether the desired API is supported by the system.

Multiple **listen-on-v6** options can be used. For example,

```
listen-on-v6 { any; };
listen-on-v6 port 1234 { !2001:db8::/32; any; };
```

will enable the name server on port 53 for any IPv6 addresses (with a single wildcard socket), and on port 1234 of IPv6 addresses that is not in the prefix 2001:db8::/32 (with separate sockets for each matched address.)

To make the server not listen on any IPv6 address, use

```
listen-on-v6 { none; };
```

If no **listen-on-v6** option is specified, the server will not listen on any IPv6 address.

10.12.1. Query Address

If the server doesn't know the answer to a question, it will query other name servers. **query-source** specifies the address and port used for such queries. For queries sent over IPv6, there is a separate **query-source-v6** option. If **address** is * (asterisk) or is omitted, a wildcard IP address (**INADDR_ANY**) will be used. If **port** is * or is omitted, a pool of random unprivileged ports will be used. See the **use-queryport-pool**, **queryport-pool-ports** and **queryport-pool-updateinterval** options below for how the pool is configured. These "queryport" options were added in BIND 9.5. The **avoid-v4-udp-ports** and **avoid-v6-udp-ports** options can be used to prevent named from selecting certain ports. The defaults are:

```
query-source address * port *;
query-source-v6 address * port *;
```

use-queryport-pool

Enable the use of query port pools. By default query port pools are enabled unless there is a explicit port defined in **query-source** or **query-source-v6**.

queryport-pool-ports

Specify how many pool ports to use. The default is 8.

queryport-pool-updateinterval

Specify how often, in minutes, that the query port pool should be recreated (new ports selected). The default is 15 minutes.

Note: The address specified in the **query-source** option is used for both UDP and TCP queries, but the port applies only to UDP queries. TCP queries always use a random unprivileged port.

Note: Solaris 2.5.1 and earlier does not support setting the source address for TCP sockets.

Also see **transfer-source** (on page 115) and **notify-source** (on page 116).

10.13. Zone Transfers

BIND has mechanisms in place to facilitate zone transfers and set limits on the amount of load that transfers place on the system. The following options apply to zone transfers.

also-notify

Defines a global list of IP addresses of name servers that are also sent NOTIFY messages whenever a fresh copy of the zone is loaded, in addition to the servers listed in the zone's NS records. This helps to ensure that copies of the zones will quickly converge on stealth servers. If an **also-notify** list is given in a **zone** statement, it will override the **options also-notify** statement. When a **zone notify** statement is set to **no**, the IP addresses in the global **also-notify** list will not be sent NOTIFY messages for that zone. The default is the empty list (no global notification list).

max-transfer-time-in

Inbound zone transfers running longer than this many minutes will be terminated. The default is 120 minutes (2 hours). The maximum value is 28 days (40320 minutes).

max-transfer-idle-in

Inbound zone transfers making no progress in this many minutes will be terminated. The default is 60 minutes (1 hour). The maximum value is 28 days (40320 minutes).

max-transfer-time-out

Outbound zone transfers running longer than this many minutes will be terminated. The default is 120 minutes (2 hours). The maximum value is 28 days (40320 minutes).

max-transfer-idle-out

Outbound zone transfers making no progress in this many minutes will be terminated. The default is 60 minutes (1 hour). The maximum value is 28 days (40320 minutes).

serial-query-rate

Slave servers will periodically query master servers to find out if zone serial numbers have changed. Each such query uses a minute amount of the slave server's network bandwidth. To limit the amount of bandwidth used, BIND 9 limits the rate at which queries are sent. The value of the **serial-query-rate** option, an integer, is the maximum number of queries sent per second. The default is 20.

serial-queries

In BIND 8, the **serial-queries** option set the maximum number of concurrent serial number queries allowed to be outstanding at any given time. BIND 9 does not limit the number of outstanding serial queries and ignores the **serial-queries** option. Instead, it limits the rate at which the queries are sent as defined using the **serial-query-rate** option.

transfer-format

Zone transfers can be sent using two different formats, **one-answer** and **many-answers**. The **transfer-format** option is used on the master server to determine which format it sends. **one-answer** uses one DNS message per resource record transferred. **many-answers** packs as many resource records as possible into a message. **many-answers** is more efficient, but is only supported by relatively new slave servers, such as BIND 9, BIND 8.x and BIND 4.9.5 onwards. The **many-answers** format is also supported by recent Microsoft Windows nameservers. The default is **many-answers**. **transfer-format** may be overridden on a per-server basis by using the **server** statement.

transfers-in

The maximum number of inbound zone transfers that can be running concurrently. The default value is 10. Increasing **transfers-in** may speed up the convergence of slave zones, but it also may increase the load on the local system.

transfers-out

The maximum number of outbound zone transfers that can be running concurrently. Zone transfer requests in excess of the limit will be refused. The default value is 10.

transfers-per-ns

The maximum number of inbound zone transfers that can be concurrently transferring from a given remote name server. The default value is 2. Increasing **transfers-per-ns** may speed up the convergence of slave zones, but it also may increase the load on the remote name server. **transfers-per-ns** may be overridden on a per-server basis by using the **transfers** phrase of the **server** statement.

transfer-source

transfer-source determines which local address will be bound to IPv4 TCP connections used to fetch zones transferred inbound by the server. It also determines the source IPv4 address, and optionally the UDP port, used for the refresh queries and forwarded dynamic updates. If not set, it defaults to a system controlled value which will usually be the address of the interface "closest to" the remote end. This address must appear in the remote end's **allow-transfer** option for the zone being transferred, if one is specified. This statement sets the **transfer-source** for all zones, but can be overridden on a per-view or per-zone basis by including a **transfer-source** statement within the **view** or **zone** block in the configuration file.

Note: Solaris 2.5.1 and earlier does not support setting the source address for TCP sockets.

transfer-source-v6

The same as **transfer-source**, except zone transfers are performed using IPv6.

alt-transfer-source

An alternate transfer source if the one listed in **transfer-source** fails and **use-alt-transfer-source** is set.

If you do not wish the alternate transfer source to be used, you should set **use-alt-transfer-source** appropriately and you should not depend upon getting a answer back to the first refresh query.

alt-transfer-source-v6

An alternate transfer source if the one listed in **transfer-source-v6** fails and **use-alt-transfer-source** is set.

use-alt-transfer-source

Use the alternate transfer sources or not. If views are specified this defaults to **no** otherwise it defaults to **yes** (for BIND 8 compatibility).

notify-source

notify-source determines which local source address, and optionally UDP port, will be used to send NOTIFY messages. This address must appear in the slave server's **masters** zone clause or in an **allow-notify** clause. This statement sets the **notify-source** for all zones, but can be overridden on a per-zone or per-view basis by including a **notify-source** statement within the **zone** or **view** block in the configuration file.

Note: Solaris 2.5.1 and earlier does not support setting the source address for TCP sockets.

notify-source-v6

Like **notify-source**, but applies to notify messages sent to IPv6 addresses.

10.14. Bad UDP Port Lists

avoid-v4-udp-ports and **avoid-v6-udp-ports** specify a list of IPv4 and IPv6 UDP ports that will not be used as system assigned source ports for UDP sockets. These lists prevent *named* from choosing as its random source port a port that is blocked by your firewall. If a query went out with such a source port, the answer would not get by the firewall and the name server would have to query again.

10.15. Operating System Resource Limits

The server's usage of many system resources can be limited. Scaled values are allowed when specifying resource limits. For example, **1G** can be used instead of **1073741824** to specify a limit of one gigabyte. **unlimited** requests unlimited use, or the maximum available amount. **default** uses the limit that was in force when the server was started. See the description of **size_spec** on page 76in section 9.1 called *Configuration File Elements*.

The following options set operating system resource limits for the name server process. Some operating systems don't support some or any of the limits. On such systems, a warning will be issued if the unsupported limit is used.

coresize

The maximum size of a core dump. The default is **default**.

datasize

The maximum amount of data memory the server may use. The default is **default**. This is a hard limit on server memory usage. If the server attempts to allocate memory in excess of this limit, the allocation will fail, which may in turn leave the server unable to perform DNS service. Therefore, this option is rarely useful as a way of limiting the amount of memory used by the server, but it can be used to raise an operating system data size limit that is too small by default. If you wish to limit the amount of memory used by the server, use the **max-cache-size** and **recursive-clients** options instead.

files

The maximum number of files the server may have open concurrently. The default is **unlimited**.

stacksize

The maximum amount of stack memory the server may use. The default is **default**.

10.16. Server Resource Limits

The following options set limits on the server's resource consumption that are enforced internally by the server rather than the operating system.

max-ixfr-log-size

This option is obsolete; it is accepted and ignored for BIND 8 compatibility. The option **max-journal-size** performs a similar function in BIND 9.

max-journal-size

Sets a maximum size for each journal file. (For more information, see section 7.3.) When the journal file approaches the specified size, some of the oldest transactions in the journal will be automatically removed. The default is **unlimited**.

host-statistics-max

In BIND 8, specifies the maximum number of host statistics entries to be kept. Not implemented in BIND 9.

recursive-clients

The maximum number of simultaneous recursive lookups the server will perform on behalf of clients. The default is 1000. Because each recursing client uses a fair bit of memory, on the order of 20 kilobytes, the value of the **recursive-clients** option may have to be decreased on hosts with limited memory.

tcp-clients

The maximum number of simultaneous client TCP connections that the server will accept. The default is 100.

max-cache-size

The maximum amount of memory to use for the server's cache, in bytes. When the amount of data in the cache reaches this limit, the server will cause records to expire prematurely so that the limit is not exceeded. In a server with multiple views, the limit applies separately to the cache of each view. The default is **unlimited**, meaning that records are purged from the cache only when their TTLs expire.

tcp-listen-queue

The listen queue depth. The default and minimum is 3. If the kernel supports the accept filter "dataready" this also controls how many TCP connections that will be queued in kernel space waiting for some data before being passed to accept. Values less than 3 will be silently raised.

10.17. Periodic Task Intervals

cleaning-interval

The server will remove expired resource records from the cache every **cleaning-interval** minutes. The default is 60 minutes. The maximum value is 28 days (40320 minutes). If set to 0, no periodic cleaning will occur.

heartbeat-interval

The server will perform zone maintenance tasks for all zones marked as **dialup** whenever this interval expires. The default is 60 minutes. Reasonable values are up to 1 day (1440 minutes). The maximum value is 28 days (40320 minutes). If set to 0, no zone maintenance for these zones will occur.

interface-interval

The server will scan the network interface list every **interface-interval** minutes. The default is 60 minutes. The maximum value is 28 days (40320 minutes). If set to 0, interface scanning will only occur when the configuration file is loaded. After the scan, the server will begin listening for queries on any newly discovered interfaces (provided they are allowed by the **listen-on** configuration), and will stop listening on interfaces that have gone away.

statistics-interval

Name server statistics will be logged every **statistics-interval** minutes. The default is 60. The maximum value is 28 days (40320 minutes). If set to 0, no statistics will be logged. (Statistics are covered in section 10.24.)

Note: Not yet implemented in BIND 9.

10.18. Topology

Note: The **topology** option is not implemented in BIND 9.

All other things being equal, when the server chooses a name server to query from a list of name servers, it prefers the one that is topologically closest to itself. The **topology** statement takes an *address_match_list* and interprets it in a special way. Each top-level list element is assigned a distance. Non-negated elements get a distance based on their position in the list, where the closer the match is to the start of the list, the shorter the distance is between it and the server. A negated match will be assigned the maximum distance from the server. If there is no match, the address will get a distance which is further than any non-negated list element, and closer than any negated element. For example,

```
topology {
    10/8;
    !1.2.3/24;
    { 1.2/16; 3/8; };
};
```

will prefer servers on network 10 the most, followed by hosts on network 1.2.0.0 (netmask 255.255.0.0) and network 3, with the exception of hosts on network 1.2.3 (netmask 255.255.255.0), which is preferred least of all.

The default topology is

```
topology { localhost; localnets; };
```

Note: The **topology** option is not implemented in BIND 9.

10.19. The sortlist Statement

The response to a DNS query may consist of multiple resource records (RRs) forming a resource records set (RRset). The name server will normally return the RRs within the RRset in an indeterminate order (but see the **rrset-order** statement in section 10.20). The client resolver code should rearrange the RRs as appropriate, that is, using any addresses on the local net in preference to other addresses. However, not all resolvers can do this or are correctly configured. When a client is using a local server, the sorting can be performed in the server, based on the client's address. This only requires configuring the name servers, not all the clients.

The **sortlist** statement (see below) takes an *address_match_list* and interprets it even more specifically than the **topology** statement does. Each top level statement in the **sortlist** must itself be an explicit *address_match_list* with one or two elements. The first element (which may be an IP address, an IP prefix, an ACL name or a nested *address_match_list*) of each top level list is checked against the source address of the query until a match is found.

Once the source address of the query has been matched, if the top level statement contains only one element, the actual primitive element that matched the source address is used to select the address in the response to move to the beginning of the response. If the statement is a list of two elements, then the second element is treated the same as the **address_match_list** in a **topology** statement. Each top level element is assigned a distance and the address in the response with the minimum distance is moved to the beginning of the response.

In the following example, any queries received from any of the addresses of the host itself will get responses preferring addresses on any of the locally connected networks. Next most preferred are addresses on the 192.168.1/24 network, and after that either the 192.168.2/24 or 192.168.3/24 network with no preference shown between these two networks. Queries received from a host on the 192.168.1/24 network will prefer other addresses on that network to the 192.168.2/24 and 192.168.3/24 networks. Queries received from a host on the 192.168.4/24 or the 192.168.5/24 network will only prefer other addresses on their directly connected networks.

```
sortlist {
    // IF   the local host
    { localhost;
        // THEN first fit on the following nets
        { localnets;
            192.168.1/24;
            { 192.168.2/24; 192.168.3/24; }; }; };
    // IF   on class C 192.168.1
    { 192.168.1/24;
        // THEN use .1, or .2 or .3
        { 192.168.1/24;
            { 192.168.2/24; 192.168.3/24; }; }; };
    // IF   on class C 192.168.2
    { 192.168.2/24;
        // THEN use .2, or .1 or .3
        { 192.168.2/24;
            { 192.168.1/24; 192.168.3/24; }; }; };
    // IF   on class C 192.168.3
```

```
    { 192.168.3/24;
        // THEN use .3, or .1 or .2
        { 192.168.3/24;
            { 192.168.1/24; 192.168.2/24; }; }; };
    // if .4 or .5, prefer that net
    { { 192.168.4/24; 192.168.5/24; };
    };
};
```

The following example will give reasonable behavior for the local host and hosts on directly connected networks. It is similar to the behavior of the address sort in BIND 4.9.x. Responses sent to queries from the local host will favor any of the directly connected networks. Responses sent to queries from any other hosts on a directly connected network will prefer addresses on that same network. Responses to other queries will not be sorted.

```
sortlist {
            { localhost; localnets; };
            { localnets; };
};
```

10.20. RRset Ordering

When multiple records are returned in an answer it may be useful to configure the order of the records placed into the response. The **rrset-order** statement permits configuration of the ordering of the records in a multiple record response. See also the **sortlist** statement in the previous section.

An *order_spec* is defined as follows:

```
[ class class_name ][ type type_name ]
  [ name "domain_name" ] order ordering
```

If no class is specified, the default is **ANY**. If no type is specified, the default is **ANY**. If no name is specified, the default is "*" (asterisk).

The legal values for **ordering** are:

fixed Records are returned in the order they are defined in the zone file. (This was implemented in BIND 9.4.)

random Records are returned in some random order.

cyclic Records are returned in a round-robin order.

For example:

```
rrset-order {
   class IN type A name "host.example.com" order random;
   order cyclic;
};
```

will cause any responses for type A records in class IN that have "*host.example.com*" as a suffix, to always be returned in random order. All other records are returned in cyclic order.

If multiple **rrset-order** statements appear, they are not combined – the last one applies.

Note: The **rrset-order** statement is not yet fully implemented in BIND 9. BIND 9 currently does not fully support "**fixed**" ordering.

10.21. Tuning

lame-ttl

Sets the number of seconds to cache a lame server indication. 0 disables caching. (This is not recommended.) The default is 600 (10 minutes) and the maximum value is 1800 (30 minutes).

max-ncache-ttl

To reduce network traffic and increase performance, the server stores negative answers. **max-ncache-ttl** is used to set a maximum retention time for these answers in the server in seconds. The default **max-ncache-ttl** is 10800 seconds (3 hours). **max-ncache-ttl** cannot exceed 7 days and will be silently truncated to 7 days if set to a greater value.

max-cache-ttl

Sets the maximum time for which the server will cache ordinary (positive) answers. The default is one week (7 days).

min-roots

The minimum number of root servers that is required for a request for the root servers to be accepted. The default is **2**.

Note: Not implemented in BIND 9.

sig-validity-interval

Specifies the number of days into the future when DNSSEC signatures automatically generated as a result of dynamic updates will expire. The default is 30 days. The maximum value is 10 years (3660 days). The signature inception time is unconditionally set to one hour before the current time to allow for a limited amount of clock skew. (For more information, see section 7.2.)

min-refresh-time, max-refresh-time, min-retry-time, max-retry-time

These options control the server's behavior on refreshing a zone (querying for SOA changes) or retrying failed transfers. Usually the SOA values for the zone are used, but these values are set by the master, giving slave server administrators little control over their contents.

These options allow the administrator to set a minimum and maximum refresh and retry time either per-zone, per-view, or globally. These options are valid for slave and stub zones, and clamp the SOA refresh and retry times to the specified values.

edns-udp-size

Sets the advertised EDNS UDP buffer size in bytes. Valid values are 512 to 4096 (values outside this range will be silently adjusted). The default value is 4096. The usual reason for setting **edns-udp-size** to a non-default value is to get UDP answers to pass through broken firewalls that block fragmented packets and/or block UDP packets that are greater than 512 bytes.

max-udp-size

Sets the maximum EDNS UDP message size named will send in bytes. Valid values are 512 to 4096 (values outside this range will be silently adjusted). The default value is 4096. The usual reason for setting **max-udp-size** to a non-default value it to get UDP answers to pass through broken firewalls that block fragmented packets and/or block UDP packets that are greater than 512 bytes. This is independent of the advertised receive buffer (**edns-udp-size**). This option was added in BIND 9.4.

masterfile-format

Specifies the file format of zone files (see chapter 11). The default value is **text**, which is the standard textual representation. Files in other formats than text are typically expected to be generated by the *named-compilezone* tool (covered in section 5.3). Note that when a zone file in a different format than text is loaded, named may omit some of the checks which would be performed for a file in the text format. In particular, **check-names** checks do not apply for the raw format.[8] This means a zone file in the **raw** format must be generated with the same check level as that specified in the named configuration file. This statement sets the **masterfile-format** for all zones, but can be overridden on a per-zone or per-view basis by including a **masterfile-format** statement within the zone or view block in the configuration file. This feature was added in BIND 9.4.

clients-per-query, max-clients-per-query

These set the initial value (minimum) and maximum number of recursive simultanious clients for any given query (<qname,qtype,qclass>) that the server will accept before dropping additional clients. named will attempt to self tune this

[8] See page 107 about the **check-names** option for details.

value and changes will be logged. The default values are 10 and 100. These options were added in BIND 9.4.

This value should reflect how many queries come in for a given name in the time it takes to resolve that name. If the number of queries exceed this value, named will assume that it is dealing with a non-responsive zone and will drop additional queries. If it gets a response after dropping queries, it will raise the estimate. The estimate will then be lowered in 20 minutes if it has remained unchanged.

If **clients-per-query** is set to zero, then there is no limit on the number of clients per query and no queries will be dropped.

If **max-clients-per-query** is set to zero, then there is no upper bound other than imposed by recursive-clients.

notify-delay

The delay, in seconds, between sending sets of notify messages for a zone. The default is 0 (zero). This feature was added in BIND 9.4.

10.22. Built-in server information zones

The server provides some helpful diagnostic information through a number of built-in zones under the pseudo-top-level-domain bind in the **CHAOS** class. These zones are part of a built-in view of class **CHAOS** which is separate from the default view of class **IN**; therefore, any global server options such as **allow-query** do not apply the these zones. If you feel the need to disable these zones, use the options below, or hide the built-in **CHAOS** view by defining an explicit view of class **CHAOS** that matches all clients.

version

The version the server should report via a query of the name *version.bind* with type **TXT**, class **CHAOS**. The default is the real version number of this server. Specifying **version none;** disables processing of the queries.

Also see section 12.3 for more details and examples.

hostname

The hostname the server should report via a query of the name *hostname.bind* with type **TXT**, class **CHAOS**. This defaults to the hostname of the machine hosting the name server as found by the gethostname() function. The primary purpose of such queries is to identify which of a group of anycast servers is actually answering your queries. Specifying **hostname none;** disables processing of the queries.

server-id

The ID of the server should report via a query of the name *ID.SERVER* with type **TXT**, class **CHAOS**. The primary purpose of such queries is to identify which of a group of anycast servers is actually answering your queries. Specifying **server-id none;** disables processing of the queries. Specifying **server-id hostname;** will cause named to use the hostname as found by the gethostname() function. The default **server-id** is **none**.

10.23. Built-in Empty Zones

named has some built-in empty zones (SOA and NS records only). These are for zones that should normally be answered locally and which queries should not be sent to the Internet's root servers. The official servers which cover these name spaces return NXDOMAIN responses to these queries. In particular, these cover the reverse name space for addresses from RFC 1918 and RFC 3330. They also include the reverse name space for IPv6 local address (locally assigned), IPv6 link local addresses, the IPv6 loopback address and the IPv6 unknown addresss.

named will attempt to determine if a built in zone already exists or is active (covered by a forward-only forwarding declaration) and will not not create a empty zone in that case.

The current list of empty zones is:

- 10.IN-ADDR.ARPA
- 127.IN-ADDR.ARPA
- 254.169.IN-ADDR.ARPA
- 16.172.IN-ADDR.ARPA
- 17.172.IN-ADDR.ARPA
- 18.172.IN-ADDR.ARPA
- 19.172.IN-ADDR.ARPA
- 20.172.IN-ADDR.ARPA
- 21.172.IN-ADDR.ARPA
- 22.172.IN-ADDR.ARPA
- 23.172.IN-ADDR.ARPA
- 24.172.IN-ADDR.ARPA
- 25.172.IN-ADDR.ARPA

- 26.172.IN-ADDR.ARPA
- 27.172.IN-ADDR.ARPA
- 28.172.IN-ADDR.ARPA
- 29.172.IN-ADDR.ARPA
- 30.172.IN-ADDR.ARPA
- 31.172.IN-ADDR.ARPA
- 168.192.IN-ADDR.ARPA
- 2.0.192.IN-ADDR.ARPA
- 0.0.0.0.0.0.0.0.0.0.0.0.0.0.0.0.0.0.0.0.0.0.0.0.0.0.0.0.0.0.0.0.IP6.ARPA
- 1.0.0.0.0.0.0.0.0.0.0.0.0.0.0.0.0.0.0.0.0.0.0.0.0.0.0.0.0.0.0.0.IP6.ARPA
- D.F.IP6.ARPA
- 8.E.F.IP6.ARPA
- 9.E.F.IP6.ARPA
- A.E.F.IP6.ARPA
- B.E.F.IP6.ARPA

Empty zones are settable at the view level and only apply to views of class IN. Disabled empty zones are only inherited from options if there are no disabled empty zones specified at the view level. To override the options list of disabled zones, you can disable the root zone at the view level, for example:

```
disable-empty-zone ".";
```

If you are using the address ranges covered here, you should already have reverse zones covering the addresses you use. In practice this appears to not be the case with many queries being made to the infrastructure servers for names in these spaces. So many in fact that sacrificial servers were needed to be deployed to channel the query load away from the infrastructure servers.

The real parent servers for these zones should disable all empty zone under the parent zone they serve. For the real root servers, this is all built in empty zones. This will enable them to return referrals to deeper in the tree.

empty-server

Specify what server name will appear in the returned SOA record for empty zones. If none is specified, then the zone's name will be used.

empty-contact

Specify what contact name will appear in the returned SOA record for empty zones. If none is specified, then "." will be used.

empty-zones-enable

Enable or disable all empty zones. By default they are enabled.

disable-empty-zone

Disable individual empty zones. By default none are disabled. This option can be specified multiple times.

These options were added in BIND 9.4.

10.24. The Statistics File

The statistics file generated by BIND 9 is similar, but not identical, to that generated by BIND 8. The statistics dump can be controlled by *rndc* (covered in section 4.3) and configured with various options. The file is located as defined by **statistics-file** (covered in section 10.8).

The statistics dump begins with a line, like:

```
+++ Statistics Dump +++ (973798949)
```

The number in parentheses is a standard Unix-style timestamp, measured as seconds since January 1, 1970.[9] Following that line are a series of lines containing a counter type, the value of the counter, optionally a zone name, and optionally a view name. The lines without view and zone listed are global statistics for the entire server. Lines with a zone and view name for the given view and zone (the view name is omitted for the default view).

The statistics dump ends with the line where the number is identical to the number in the beginning line; for example:

```
--- Statistics Dump --- (973798949)
```

The following statistics counters are maintained:

success The number of successful queries made to the server or zone. A successful query is defined as query which returns a NOERROR response with at least one answer RR.

[9] On a BSD system, this can be converted with "`date -r`".

referral The number of queries which resulted in referral responses.

nxrrset The number of queries which resulted in NOERROR responses with no data.

nxdomain The number of queries which resulted in NXDOMAIN responses.

failure The number of queries which resulted in a failure response other than those above.

recursion The number of queries which caused the server to perform recursion in order to find the final answer.

duplicate The number of queries which caused the server to perform recursion in order to find the final answer.

dropped The number of queries for which the server discovered an excessive number of existing recursive queries for the same name, type and class – and were subsequently dropped.

Each query received by the server will cause exactly one of **success**, **referral**, **nxrrset**, **nxdomain**, or **failure** to be incremented, and may additionally cause the **recursion** counter to be incremented.

Example

```
# rndc stats
# tail named.stats
+++ Statistics Dump +++ (1188845591)
success 67286553
referral 343494
nxrrset 1849038
nxdomain 11217173
recursion 3294610
failure 748659
duplicate 27626
dropped 2754
--- Statistics Dump --- (1188845591)
# date -r 1188845591
Mon Sep  3 11:53:11 PDT 2007
```

Stats in XML format are also available; see the **stats-server** option on page 99.

10.25. Additional Section Caching

The additional section cache, also called **acache**, is an internal cache to improve the response performance of BIND 9. When additional section caching is enabled, BIND 9 will cache an internal short-cut to the additional section content for each answer RR. Note that acache is an internal caching mechanism of BIND 9, and is not related to the DNS caching server function.

Additional section caching does not change the response content (except the RRsets ordering of the additional section, see below), but can improve the response performance significantly. It is particularly effective when BIND 9 acts as an authoritative server for a zone that has many delegations with many glue RRs.

In order to obtain the maximum performance improvement from additional section caching, setting **additional-from-cache** to **no** is recommended, since the current implementation of acache does not short-cut of additional section information from the DNS cache data.

One obvious disadvantage of acache is that it requires much more memory for the internal cached data. Thus, if the response performance does not matter and memory consumption is much more critical, the acache mechanism can be disabled by setting **acache-enable** to **no**. It is also possible to specify the upper limit of memory consumption for acache by using **max-acache-size**.

Additional section caching also has a minor effect on the RRset ordering in the additional section. Without **acache**, **cyclic** order is effective for the additional section as well as the answer and authority sections. However, additional section caching fixes the ordering when it first caches an RRset for the additional section, and the same ordering will be kept in succeeding responses, regardless of the setting of **rrset-order**. The effect of this should be minor, however, since an RRset in the additional section typically only contains a small number of RRs (and in many cases it only contains a single RR), in which case the ordering does not matter much.

The following is a summary of options related to acache.

acache-enable

If **yes**, additional section caching is enabled. The default value is **no**. This option was added in BIND 9.4.

acache-cleaning-interval

The server will remove stale cache entries, based on an LRU based algorithm, every **acache-cleaning-interval** minutes. The default is 60 minutes. If set to 0, no periodic cleaning will occur. This option was added in BIND 9.4.

max-acache-size

The maximum amount of memory in bytes to use for the server's acache. When the amount of data in the acache reaches this limit, the server will clean more aggressively so that the limit is not exceeded. In a server with multiple views, the limit applies separately to the acache of each view. The default is **unlimited**, meaning that entries are purged from the acache only at the periodic cleaning time. This feature was added in BIND 9.4.

10.26. server Statement

server Statement Grammar

```
server ip_addr[/prefixlen] {
    [ bogus yes_or_no ; ]
    [ provide-ixfr yes_or_no ; ]
    [ request-ixfr yes_or_no ; ]
    [ edns yes_or_no ; ]
    [ edns-udp-size number ; ]
    [ max-udp-size number ; ]
    [ transfers number ; ]
    [ transfer-format
       ( one-answer | many-answers ) ; ]]
    [ keys { string ; [ string ; [...]] } ; ]
    [ transfer-source
      (ip4_addr | *) [port ip_port] ; ]
    [ transfer-source-v6
      (ip6_addr | *) [port ip_port] ; ]
    [ notify-source (ip4_addr | *) [port ip_port] ; ]
    [ notify-source-v6
      (ip6_addr | *) [port ip_port] ; ]
    [ query-source [ address
      ( ip_addr | * ) ] [ port (  ip_port | * ) ]; ]
    [ query-source-v6 [ address
      ( ip_addr | * ) ] [ port ( ip_port | * ) ]; ]
    [ use-queryport-pool yes_or_no; ]
    [ queryport-pool-ports number; ]
    [ queryport-pool-interval number; ]
};
```

server Statement Definition and Usage

The **server** statement defines characteristics to be associated with a remote name server. If a prefix length is specified, then a range of servers is covered. Only the most specific server clause applies regardless of the order in *named.conf*.

The **server** statement can occur at the top level of the configuration file or inside a **view** statement. If a **view** statement contains one or more **server** statements, only those apply to the view and any top-level ones are ignored. If a view contains no **server** statements, any top-level **server** statements are used as defaults.

If you discover that a remote server is giving out bad data, marking it as bogus will prevent further queries to it. The default value of **bogus** is **no**.

The **provide-ixfr** clause determines whether the local server, acting as master, will respond with an incremental zone transfer when the given remote server, a slave, requests it. If set to **yes**, incremental transfer will be provided whenever possible. If set to **no**, all transfers to the remote server will be non-incremental. If not set, the value of the **provide-ixfr** option in the view or global options block is used as a default.

The **request-ixfr** clause determines whether the local server, acting as a slave, will request incremental zone transfers from the given remote server, a master. If not set, the value of the **request-ixfr** option in the view or global options block is used as a default.

IXFR requests to servers that do not support IXFR will automatically fall back to AXFR. Therefore, there is no need to manually list which servers support IXFR and which ones do not; the global default of **yes** should always work. The purpose of the **provide-ixfr** and **request-ixfr** clauses is to make it possible to disable the use of IXFR even when both master and slave claim to support it, for example if one of the servers is buggy and crashes or corrupts data when IXFR is used.

The **edns** clause determines whether the local server will attempt to use EDNS (Extension Mechanisms for DNS) when communicating with the remote server. The default is **yes**.

The **edns-udp-size** option sets the EDNS UDP size that is advertised by named when querying the remote server. Valid values are 512 to 4096 bytes (values outside this range will be silently adjusted). This option is useful when you wish to advertises a different value to this server than the value you advertise globally, for example, when there is a firewall at the remote site that is blocking large replies.

The **max-udp-size** option sets the maximum EDNS UDP message size named will send. Valid values are 512 to 4096 bytes (values outside this range will be silently adjusted). This option is useful when you know that there is a firewall that is blocking large replies from *named*. This option was added in BIND 9.4.

The server supports two zone transfer methods. The first, **one-answer**, uses one DNS message per resource record transferred. **many-answers** packs as many resource records as possible into a message. **many-answers** is more efficient, but is only known to be understood by BIND 9, BIND 8.x, and patched versions of BIND 4.9.5. You can specify which method to use for a server with the **transfer-format** option. If **transfer-format** is not specified, the **transfer-format** specified by the **options** statement will be used. (See page 114 for details.)

transfers is used to limit the number of concurrent inbound zone transfers from the specified server. If no **transfers** clause is specified, the limit is set according to the **transfers-per-ns** option.

The **keys** clause identifies a **key_id** defined by the **key** statement, to be used for transaction security (TSIG) when talking to the remote server. When a request is sent to the remote server, a request signature will be generated using the key specified here and appended to the message. A request originating from the remote server is not required to be signed by this key. (See section 7.6 for information about TSIG.)

Although the grammar of the **keys** clause allows for multiple keys, only a single key per server is currently supported.

The **transfer-source** and **transfer-source-v6** clauses specify the IPv4 and IPv6 source address to be used for zone transfer with the remote server, respectively. For an IPv4 remote server, only **transfer-source** can be specified. Similarly, for an IPv6 remote server, only **transfer-source-v6** can be specified. For more details, see the description of **transfer-source** and **transfer-source-v6** on page 115in the *Zone Transfers* section 10.13.

The **notify-source** and **notify-source-v6** clauses specify the IPv4 and IPv6 source address to be used for notify messages sent to remote servers, respectively. For an IPv4 remote server, only **notify-source** can be specified. Similarly, for an IPv6 remote server, only **notify-source-v6** can be specified. (Support for this to be specified on a per server basis was added in BIND 9.4.) For more details, see page 116.

The **query-source** and **query-source-v6** clauses specify the IPv4 and IPv6 source address to be used for queries sent to remote servers, respectively. For an IPv4 remote server, only **query-source** can be specified. Similarly, for an IPv6 remote server, only **query-source-v6** can be specified. (Support for this to be specified on a per server basis was added in BIND 9.4.)

10.27. trusted-keys Statement

trusted-keys Statement Grammar

```
trusted-keys {
    string number number number string ;
    [ string number number number string ; [...]]
};
```

trusted-keys Statement Definition and Usage

The **trusted-keys** statement defines DNSSEC security roots. DNSSEC is described in section 7.9. A security root is defined when the public key for a non-authoritative zone is known, but cannot be securely obtained through DNS, either because it is the DNS root zone or because its parent zone is unsigned. Once a key has been configured as a trusted key, it is treated as if it had been validated and proven secure. The resolver attempts DNSSEC validation on all DNS data in subdomains of a security root.

All keys (and corresponding zones) listed in **trusted-keys** are deemed to exist regardless of what parent zones say. Similarly for all keys listed in trusted-keys only those keys are used to validate the DNSKEY RRset. The parent's DS RRset will not be used.

The **trusted-keys** statement can contain multiple key entries, each consisting of the key's domain name, flags, protocol, algorithm, and the Base-64 representation of the key data.

10.28. view Statement

view Statement Grammar

```
view view_name
      [class] {
      match-clients { address_match_list };
      match-destinations { address_match_list };
      match-recursive-only yes_or_no ;
      [ view_option; ...]
      [ zone_statement; ...]
};
```

view Statement Definition and Usage

The **view** statement is a powerful feature of BIND 9 that lets a name server answer a DNS query differently depending on who is asking. It is particularly useful for implementing split DNS setups without having to run multiple servers.

Each **view** statement defines a view of the DNS name space that will be seen by a subset of clients. A client matches a view if its source IP address matches the address_match_list of the view's **match-clients** clause and its destination IP address matches the address_match_list of the view's **match-destinations** clause. If not specified, both **match-clients** and **match-destinations** default to matching all addresses. In addition to checking IP addresses **match-clients** and **match-destinations** can also take **keys** which provide an mechanism for the client to select the view. A view can also be specified as **match-recursive-only**, which means that only recursive requests from matching clients will match that view. The order of the **view** statements is significant – a client request will be resolved in the context of the first **view** that it matches.

Zones defined within a **view** statement will be only be accessible to clients that match the **view**. By defining a zone of the same name in multiple views, different zone data can be given to different clients, for example, "internal" and "external" clients in a split DNS setup.

Many of the options given in the **options** statement can also be used within a **view** statement, and then apply only when resolving queries with that view. When no view-specific value is given, the value in the **options** statement is used as a default. Also, zone options can have default values specified in the **view** statement; these view-specific defaults take precedence over those in the **options** statement.

Views are class specific. If no class is given, class IN is assumed. Note that all non-IN views must contain a hint zone, since only the IN class has compiled-in default hints.

If there are no **view** statements in the config file, a default view that matches any client is automatically created in class IN. Any **zone** statements specified on the top level of the configuration file are considered to be part of this default view, and the **options** statement will apply to the default view. If any explicit **view** statements are present, all **zone** statements must occur inside **view** statements.

Here is an example of a typical split DNS setup implemented using **view** statements:

```
view "internal" {
      // This should match our internal networks.
      match-clients { 10.0.0.0/8; };

      // Provide recursive service to internal
      // clients only.
      recursion yes;

      // Provide a complete view of the example.com
      // zone including addresses of internal hosts.
      zone "example.com" {
            type master;
            file "example-internal.db";
      };
};

view "external" {
      // Match all clients not matched by the
      // previous view.
      match-clients { any; };

      // Refuse recursive service to external clients.
      recursion no;

      // Provide a restricted view of the example.com
      // zone containing only publicly accessible hosts.
      zone "example.com" {
           type master;
           file "example-external.db";
      };
};
```

10.29. zone Statement

zone Statement Grammar

```
zone zone_name [class] {
    type master;
    [ allow-query { address_match_list }; ]
    [ allow-query-on { address_match_list }; ]
```

```
    [ allow-transfer { address_match_list }; ]
    [ allow-update { address_match_list }; ]
    [ update-policy { update_policy_rule [...] }; ]
    [ also-notify { ip_addr [port ip_port] ;
      [ ip_addr [port ip_port] ; ... ] }; ]
    [ check-names (warn | fail | ignore ) ; ]
    [ check-mx ( warn | fail | ignore ) ; ]
    [ check-wildcard yes_or_no; ]
    [ check-integrity yes_or_no ; ]
    [ dialup dialup_option ; ]
    [ file string ; ]
    [ masterfile-format ( text | raw ) ; ]
    [ journal string ; ]
    [ forward ( only | first ) ; ]
    [ forwarders {
      [ ip_addr [port ip_port] ; ... ] }; ]
    [ ixfr-base string ; ]
    [ ixfr-tmp-file string ; ]
    [ maintain-ixfr-base yes_or_no ; ]
    [ max-ixfr-log-size number ; ]
    [ max-transfer-idle-out number ; ]
    [ max-transfer-time-out number ; ]
    [ notify
      yes_or_no | explicit | master-only ; ]
    [ notify seconds ; ]
    [ pubkey number number number string ; ]
    [ notify-source (ip4_addr | *) [port ip_port] ; ]
    [ notify-source-v6
      (ip6_addr | *) [port ip_port] ; ]
    [ zone-statistics yes_or_no ; ]
    [ sig-validity-interval number ; ]
    [ database string ; ]
    [ min-refresh-time number ; ]
    [ max-refresh-time number ; ]
    [ min-retry-time number ; ]
    [ max-retry-time number ; ]
    [ key-directory path_name; ]
    [ zero-no-soa-ttl yes_or_no ; ]
};
zone zone_name [class] {
    type slave;
    [ allow-notify { address_match_list }; ]
    [ allow-query { address_match_list }; ]
    [ allow-query-on { address_match_list }; ]
    [ allow-transfer { address_match_list }; ]
```

```
[ allow-update-forwarding {
   address_match_list }; ]
[ update-check-ksk yes_or_no; ]
[ try-tcp-refresh yes_or_no; ]
[ also-notify { ip_addr [port ip_port] ;
  [ ip_addr [port ip_port] ; ... ] }; ]
[ check-names ( warn | fail | ignore ) ; ]
[ dialup dialup_option ; ]
[ file string ; ]
[ masterfile-format ( text | raw ) ; ]
[ journal string ; ]
[ forward ( only | first ) ; ]
[ forwarders {
  [ ip_addr [port ip_port] ; ... ] }; ]
[ ixfr-base string ; ]
[ ixfr-tmp-file string ; ]
[ maintain-ixfr-base yes_or_no ; ]
[ masters [port ip_port] {
  ( masters_list | ip_addr [port ip_port] [key key] ) ;
  [...] }; ]
[ max-ixfr-log-size number ; ]
[ max-transfer-idle-in number ; ]
[ max-transfer-idle-out number ; ]
[ max-transfer-time-in number ; ]
[ max-transfer-time-out number ; ]
[ notify yes_or_no | explicit | master-only ; ]
[ pubkey number number number string ; ]
[ transfer-source
  (ip4_addr | *) [port ip_port] ; ]
[ transfer-source-v6
  (ip6_addr | *) [port ip_port] ; ]
[ alt-transfer-source
  (ip4_addr | *) [port ip_port] ; ]
[ alt-transfer-source-v6
  (ip6_addr | *) [port ip_port] ; ]
[ use-alt-transfer-source yes_or_no; ]
[ notify-source (ip4_addr | *) [port ip_port] ; ]
[ notify-source-v6 (ip6_addr | *) [port ip_port] ; ]
[ zone-statistics yes_or_no ; ]
[ database string ; ]
[ min-refresh-time number ; ]
[ max-refresh-time number ; ]
[ min-retry-time number ; ]
[ max-retry-time number ; ]
[ multi-master yes_or_no ; ]
```

```
    [ zero-no-soa-ttl yes_or_no ; ]
};
zone zone_name [class] {
    type hint;
    file string ;
    [ delegation-only yes_or_no ; ]
    [ check-names ( warn | fail | ignore ) ; 10 ]
};
zone zone_name [class] {
    type stub;
    [ allow-query { address_match_list }; ]
    [ allow-query-on { address_match_list }; ]
    [ check-names ( warn | fail | ignore) ; ]
    [ dialup dialup_option ; ]
    [ delegation-only yes_or_no ; ]
    [ file string ; ]
    [ masterfile-format ( text | raw ) ; ]
    [ forward ( only | first ) ; ]
    [ forwarders {
      [ ip_addr [port ip_port] ; ... ] }; ]
    [ masters [port ip_port] {
      ( masters_list | ip_addr [port ip_port] [key key] ) ;
      [...] }; ]
    [ max-transfer-idle-in number ; ]
    [ max-transfer-time-in number ; ]
    [ pubkey number number number string ; ]
    [ transfer-source
      (ip4_addr | *) [port ip_port] ; ]
    [ transfer-source-v6
      (ip6_addr | *) [port ip_port] ; ]
    [ alt-transfer-source
      (ip4_addr | *) [port ip_port] ; ]
    [ alt-transfer-source-v6
      (ip6_addr | *) [port ip_port] ; ]
    [ use-alt-transfer-source yes_or_no; ]
    [ zone-statistics yes_or_no ; ]
    [ database string ; ]
    [ min-refresh-time number ; ]
    [ max-refresh-time number ; ]
    [ min-retry-time number ; ]
    [ max-retry-time number ; ]
    [ multi-master yes_or_no ; ]
};
zone zone_name [class] {
```

[10] **check-names** is not implemented.

```
    type forward;
    [ forward ( only | first ) ; ]
    [ forwarders {
      [ ip_addr [port ip_port] ; ... ] }; ]
    [ delegation-only yes_or_no ; ]
};
zone zone_name [class] {
    type delegation-only;
};
```

zone Statement Definition and Usage

Zone Types

master The server has a master copy of the data for the zone and will be able to provide authoritative answers for it.

slave A slave zone is a replica of a master zone. The **masters** list specifies one or more IP addresses of master servers that the slave contacts to update its copy of the zone. Masters list elements can also be names of other **masters** lists. By default, transfers are made from port 53 on the servers; this can be changed for all servers by specifying a port number before the list of IP addresses, or on a per-server basis after the IP address. Authentication to the master can also be done with per-server TSIG keys.

If a **file** is specified, then the replica will be written to this file whenever the zone is changed, and reloaded from this file on a server restart. Use of a file is recommended, since it often speeds server startup and eliminates a needless waste of bandwidth.

Note that for large numbers (in the tens or hundreds of thousands) of zones per server, it is best to use a two-level naming scheme for zone filenames. For example, a slave server for the zone example.com might place the zone contents into a file called *ex/example.com* where *ex/* is just the first two letters of the zone name. (Most operating systems behave very slowly if you put 100,000 files into a single directory.)

stub A stub zone is similar to a slave zone, except that it replicates only the NS records of a master zone instead of the entire zone. Stub zones are not a standard part of the DNS; they are a feature specific to the BIND implementation. Stub zones can be used to eliminate the need for glue NS record in a parent zone at the expense of maintaining a stub zone entry and a set of name server addresses in named.conf. This usage is not recommended for new configurations, and BIND 9 supports it only in a limited way. In BIND 4/8, zone transfers of a parent zone included the NS records from stub children of that zone. This meant that, in some cases, users could get away with configuring child stubs only in the master server for the parent zone. BIND 9 never mixes together zone data from different zones in this way. Therefore, if a BIND 9 master serving a parent zone has child stub zones configured, all the slave servers for the parent zone also need to have the same child stub zones configured.

Stub zones can also be used as a way of forcing the resolution of a given domain to use a particular set of authoritative servers. For example, the caching name servers on a private network using RFC 1918 addressing may be configured with stub zones for 10.in-addr.arpa to use a set of internal name servers as the authoritative servers for that domain.

forward A "forward zone" is a way to configure forwarding on a per-domain basis. A **zone** statement of **type forward** can contain a **forward** and/or **forwarders** statement, which will apply to queries within the domain given by the zone name. If no **forwarders** statement is present or an empty list for **forwarders** is given, then no forwarding will be done for the domain, canceling the effects of any **forwarders** in the **options** statement. Thus if you want to use this type of zone to change the behavior of the global **forward** option (that is, "**forward first**" to, then "**forward only**", or vice versa, but want to use the same servers as set globally) you need to re-specify the global **forwarders**.

hint The initial set of root name servers is specified using a "hint zone". When the server starts up, it uses the root hints to find a root name server and get the most recent list of root name servers. If no hint zone is specified for class IN, the server uses a compiled-in default set of root servers hints. Classes other than IN have no built-in defaults hints.

delegation-only This is used to enforce the delegation-only status of infrastructure zones (e.g. COM, NET, ORG). Any answer that is received without an explicit or implicit delegation in the authority section will be treated as NXDOMAIN. This does not apply to the zone apex. This should not be applied to leaf zones. **delegation-only** has no effect on answers received from forwarders.

Class

The zone's name may optionally be followed by a class. If a class is not specified, **class IN** (for Internet), is assumed. This is correct for the vast majority of cases.

The hesiod class is named for an information service from MIT's Project Athena. It is used to share information about various systems databases, such as users, groups, printers and so on. The keyword HS is a synonym for hesiod.

Another MIT development is Chaosnet, a LAN protocol created in the mid-1970s. Zone data for it can be specified with the CHAOS class.

Zone Options

allow-notify

See the description of **allow-notify** on page 109 in section 10.11 called *Access Control*.

allow-query

See the description of **allow-query** in the *Access Control* section 10.11.

allow-query-on

See the description of **allow-query-on** in the *Access Control* section 10.11.

allow-transfer

See the description of **allow-transfer** on page 111in the *Access Control* section 10.11.

allow-update

See the description of **allow-update** in the Access Control section (page 109).

update-policy

Specifies a "Simple Secure Update" policy. See the section called *Dynamic Update Policies* on page 144.

allow-update-forwarding

See the description of **allow-update-forwarding** in the section called *Access Control* on page 109.

also-notify

Only meaningful if **notify** is active for this zone. The set of machines that will receive a DNS NOTIFY message for this zone is made up of all the listed name servers (other than the primary master) for the zone plus any IP addresses specified with **also-notify**. A port may be specified with each **also-notify** address to send the notify messages to a port other than the default of 53. **also-notify** is not meaningful for stub zones. The default is the empty list.

check-names

This option is used to restrict the character set and syntax of certain domain names in master files and/or DNS responses received from the network. The default varies according to zone type. For **master** zones the default is **fail**. For **slave** zones the default is **warn**.

check-mx

See the description of **check-mx** in the Boolean Options section (page 102).

check-wildcard

See the description of **check-wildcard** in the Boolean Options section (page 102).

check-integrity

See the description of **check-integrity** in the Boolean Options section (page 102).

check-sibling

See the description of **check-sibling** in the Boolean Options section (page 102).

zero-no-soa-ttl

See the description of **zero-no-soa-ttl** in the Boolean Options section (page 102).

update-check-ksk

See the description of **update-check-ksk** in the Boolean Options section (page 102).

try-tcp-refresh

See the description of **try-tcp-refresh** in the Boolean Options section (page 102).

database

Specify the type of database to be used for storing the zone data. The string following the **database** keyword is interpreted as a list of whitespace-delimited words. The first word identifies the database type, and any subsequent words are passed as arguments to the database to be interpreted in a way specific to the database type.

The default is **"rbt"**, BIND 9's native in-memory red-black-tree database. This database does not take arguments.

Other values are possible if additional database drivers have been linked into the server. Some sample drivers are included with the distribution but none are linked in by default.

dialup

See the description of **dialup** in the section called *Boolean Options* on page 102.

delegation-only

The flag only applies to hint and stub zones. If set to **yes**, then the zone will also be treated as if it is also a delegation-only type zone.

forward

Only meaningful if the zone has a **forwarders** list. The **only** value causes the lookup to fail after trying the forwarders and getting no answer, while **first** would allow a normal lookup to be tried.

forwarders

Used to override the list of global **forwarders**. If it is not specified in a zone of type **forward**, no forwarding is done for the zone and the global options are not used.

ixfr-base

Was used in BIND 8 to specify the name of the transaction log (journal) file for dynamic update and IXFR. BIND 9 ignores the option and constructs the name of the journal file by appending "*.jnl*" to the name of the zone file.

ixfr-tmp-file

Was an undocumented option in BIND 8. Ignored in BIND 9.

journal

Allow the default journal's filename to be overridden. The default is the zone's filename with `".jnl"` appended. This is applicable to **master** and **slave** zones. This setting was added in BIND 9.4.

max-transfer-time-in

See the description of **max-transfer-time-in** in section 10.13 called *Zone Transfers*.

max-transfer-idle-in

See the description of **max-transfer-idle-in** in section 10.13 called *Zone Transfers*.

max-transfer-time-out

See the description of **max-transfer-time-out** in section 10.13 called *Zone Transfers*.

max-transfer-idle-out

See the description of **max-transfer-idle-out** in section 10.13 called *Zone Transfers*.

notify

See the description of **notify** in the section called *Boolean Options* (page 102).

notify-delay

See the description of **notify-delay** in the section called *Tuning* (page 122).

pubkey

In BIND 8, this option was intended for specifying a public zone key for verification of signatures in DNSSEC signed zones when they are loaded from disk. BIND 9 does not verify signatures on load and ignores the option.

zone-statistics

If **yes**, the server will keep statistical information for this zone, which can be dumped to the **statistics-file** defined in the server options. See section 10.8 for more details.

sig-validity-interval

See the description of **sig-validity-interval** in section 10.21 called *Tuning*.

transfer-source

See the description of **transfer-source** on page 115in section 10.13 called *Zone Transfers*.

transfer-source-v6

See the description of **transfer-source-v6** in section 10.13 called *Zone Transfers*.

alt-transfer-source

See the description of **alt-transfer-source** in section 10.13 called *Zone Transfers*.

alt-transfer-source-v6

See the description of **alt-transfer-source-v6** in section 10.13 called *Zone Transfers*.

use-alt-transfer-source

See the description of **use-alt-transfer-source** in section 10.13 called *Zone Transfers*.

notify-source

See the description of **notify-source** on page 116in section 10.13 called *Zone Transfers*.

notify-source-v6

See the description of **notify-source-v6** in section 10.13 called *Zone Transfers*.

min-refresh-time, max-refresh-time, min-retry-time, max-retry-time

See the description in section 10.21 called *Tuning*.

ixfr-from-differences

See the description of **ixfr-from-differences** in the section called *Boolean Options* (page 102).

key-directory

See the description of **key-directory** in section 10.8 called *options Statement Definition and Usage*.

multi-master

See the description of **multi-master** in the section called *Boolean Options* (page 102).

masterfile-format

See the description of **masterfile-format** in the *Boolean Options* section (page 102).

10.30. Dynamic Update Policies

BIND 9 supports two alternative methods of granting clients the right to perform dynamic updates to a zone, configured by the **allow-update** and **update-policy** option, respectively.

The **allow-update** clause works the same way as in previous versions of BIND. It grants given clients the permission to update any record of any name in the zone.

The **update-policy** clause is new in BIND 9 and allows more fine-grained control over what updates are allowed. A set of rules is specified, where each rule either grants or denies permissions for one or more names to be updated by one or more identities. If the dynamic update request message is signed (that is, it includes either a TSIG or SIG(0) record), the identity of the signer can be determined.

Rules are specified in the **update-policy** zone option, and are only meaningful for master zones. When the **update-policy** statement is present, it is a configuration error for the **allow-update** statement to be present. The **update-policy** statement only examines the signer of a message; the source address is not relevant.

This is how a rule definition looks:

```
( grant | deny ) identity nametype name [ types ]
```

Each rule grants or denies privileges. Once a message has successfully matched a rule, the operation is immediately granted or denied and no further rules are examined. A rule is matched when the signer matches the identity field, the name matches the name field in accordance with the nametype field, and the type matches the types specified in the type field.

The identity field specifies a name or a wildcard name. Normally, this is the name of the TSIG or SIG(0) key used to sign the update request. When a TKEY exchange has been used to create a shared secret, the identity of the shared secret is the same as the identity of the key used to authenticate the TKEY exchange. TKEY is also the negotiation method used by GSS-TSIG, which establishes an identity that is the Kerberos principal of the client, such as "user@host.domain". When the *identity* field specifies a wildcard name, it is subject to DNS wildcard expansion, so the rule will apply to multiple identities. The *identity* field must contain a fully-qualified domain name.

The *nametype* field has 6 values: name, subdomain, wildcard, self, selfsub, and selfwild.

name Exact-match semantics. This rule matches when the name being updated is identical to the contents of the name field.

subdomain This rule matches when the name being updated is a subdomain of, or identical to, the contents of the name field.

wildcard The name field is subject to DNS wildcard expansion, and this rule matches when the name being updated name is a valid expansion of the wildcard.

self This rule matches when the name being updated matches the contents of the identity field. The name field is ignored, but should be the same as the identity field. The **self** nametype is most useful when allowing using one key per name to update, where the key has the same name as the name to be updated. The identity would be specified as * (an asterisk) in this case.

selfsub This rule is similar to self except that subdomains of self can also be updated. This was added in BIND 9.4.

selfwild This rule is similar to self except that only subdomains of self can be updated. This was added in BIND 9.4.

In all cases, the *name* field must specify a fully-qualified domain name.

If no types are explicitly specified, this rule matches all types except RRSIG, NS, SOA, and NSEC. Types may be specified by name, including "ANY" (ANY matches all types except NSEC, which can never be updated). Note that when an attempt is made to delete all records associated with a name, the rules are checked for each existing record type.

11. Zone Files

11.1. Using Resource Records

This chapter, largely borrowed from RFC 1034, describes the concept of a Resource Record (RR) and explains when each is used. Since the publication of RFC 1034, several new RRs have been identified and implemented in the DNS. These are also included.

11.1.1. Resource Records

A domain name identifies a node. Each node has a set of resource information, which may be empty. The set of resource information associated with a particular name is composed of separate RRs. The order of RRs in a set is not significant and need not be preserved by name servers, resolvers, or other parts of the DNS. However, sorting of multiple RRs is permitted for optimization purposes, for example, to specify that a particular nearby server be tried first. See the section called *The sortlist Statement* on page 119 and the section called *RRset Ordering* on page 121.

The components of a Resource Record are:

owner name The domain name where the RR is found.

type An encoded 16-bit value that specifies the type of the resource record.

TTL The time-to-live of the RR. This field is a 32-bit integer in units of seconds, and is primarily used by resolvers when they cache RRs. The TTL describes how long a RR can be cached before it should be discarded.

class An encoded 16-bit value that identifies a protocol family or instance of a protocol.

RDATA The resource data. The format of the data is type (and sometimes class) specific.

The following are *types* of valid RRs:

A A host address. In the IN class, this is a 32-bit IP address. Described in RFC 1035.

AAAA IPv6 address. Described in RFC 1886.

A6 IPv6 address. This can be a partial address (a suffix) and an indirection to the name where the rest of the address (the prefix) can be found. Experimental. Described in RFC 2874.

AFSDB Location of AFS database servers. Experimental. Described in RFC 1183.

APL Address prefix list. Experimental. Described in RFC 3123.

CERT Holds a digital certificate. Described in RFC 2538.

CNAME Identifies the canonical name of an alias. Described in RFC 1035.

DNAME Replaces the domain name specified with another name to be looked up, effectively aliasing an entire subtree of the domain name space rather than a single record as in the case of the CNAME RR. Described in RFC 2672.

DNSKEY Stores a public key associated with a signed DNS zone. Described in RFC 4034.

DS Stores the hash of a public key associated with a signed DNS zone. Described in RFC 4034.

GPOS Specifies the global position. Superseded by LOC.

HINFO Identifies the CPU and OS used by a host. Described in RFC 1035.

ISDN Representation of ISDN addresses. Experimental. Described in RFC 1183.

KEY Stores a public key associated with a DNS name. Used in original DNSSEC; replaced by DNSKEY in DNSSECbis, but still used with SIG(0). Described in RFCs 2535 and 2931.

KX Identifies a key exchanger for this DNS name. Described in RFC 2230.

LOC For storing GPS info. Described in RFC 1876. Experimental.

MX Identifies a mail exchange for the domain with a 16-bit preference value (lower is better) followed by the host name of the mail exchange. Described in RFC 974, RFC 1035. See section 11.1.3 in this book.

NAPTR Name authority pointer. Described in RFC 2915.

NSAP A network service access point. Described in RFC 1706.

NS The authoritative name server for the domain. Described in RFC 1035.

NSEC Used in DNSSECbis to securely indicate that RRs with an owner name in a certain name interval do not exist in a zone and indicate what RR types are present for an existing name. Described in RFC 4034.

NXT Used in DNSSEC to securely indicate that RRs with an owner name in a certain name interval do not exist in a zone and indicate what RR types are present for an existing name. Used in original DNSSEC; replaced by NSEC in DNSSECbis. Described in RFC 2535.

PTR A pointer to another part of the domain name space. Described in RFC 1035. See section 11.1.6 in this book.

PX Provides mappings between RFC 822 and X.400 addresses. Described in RFC 2163.

RP Information on persons responsible for the domain. Experimental. Described in RFC 1183.

RRSIG Contains DNSSECbis signature data. Described in RFC 4034.

RT Route-through binding for hosts that do not have their own direct wide area network addresses. Experimental. Described in RFC 1183.

SIG Contains DNSSEC signature data. Used in original DNSSEC; replaced by RRSIG in DNSSECbis, but still used for SIG(0). Described in RFCs 2535 and 2931.

SOA Identifies the start of a zone of authority. Described in RFC 1035.

SRV Information about well known network services (replaces WKS). Described in RFC 2782.

TXT Text records. Described in RFC 1035.

WKS Information about which well known network services, such as SMTP, that a domain supports. Historical.

X25 Representation of X.25 network addresses. Experimental. Described in RFC 1183.

The following *classes* of resource records are currently valid in the DNS:

IN The Internet.

CH Chaosnet, a LAN protocol created at MIT in the mid-1970s. Rarely used for its historical purpose, but reused for BIND's built-in server information zones, e.g., *version.bind*.[1]

HS Hesiod, an information service developed by MIT's Project Athena. It is used to share information about various systems databases, such as users, groups, printers and so on.

[1] See page 124 about *version.bind*.

The owner name is often implicit, rather than forming an integral part of the RR. For example, many name servers internally form tree or hash structures for the name space, and chain RRs off nodes. The remaining RR parts are the fixed header (type, class, TTL) which is consistent for all RRs, and a variable part (RDATA) that fits the needs of the resource being described.

The meaning of the TTL field is a time limit on how long an RR can be kept in a cache. This limit does not apply to authoritative data in zones; it is also timed out, but by the refreshing policies for the zone. The TTL is assigned by the administrator for the zone where the data originates. While short TTLs can be used to minimize caching, and a zero TTL prohibits caching, the realities of Internet performance suggest that these times should be on the order of days for the typical host. If a change can be anticipated, the TTL can be reduced prior to the change to minimize inconsistency during the change, and then increased back to its former value following the change.

The data in the RDATA section of RRs is carried as a combination of binary strings and domain names. The domain names are frequently used as "pointers" to other data in the DNS.

11.1.2. Textual expression of RRs

RRs are represented in binary form in the packets of the DNS protocol, and are usually represented in highly encoded form when stored in a name server or resolver. In the examples provided in RFC 1034, a style similar to that used in master files was employed in order to show the contents of RRs. In this format, most RRs are shown on a single line, although continuation lines are possible using parentheses.

The start of the line gives the owner of the RR. If a line begins with a blank, then the owner is assumed to be the same as that of the previous RR. Blank lines are often included for readability.

Following the owner, the TTL, type, and class of the RR are listed. Class and type use the mnemonics defined above, and TTL is an integer before the type field. In order to avoid ambiguity in parsing, type and class mnemonics are disjoint, TTLs are integers, and the type mnemonic is always last. The IN class and TTL values are often omitted from examples in the interests of clarity.

The resource data or RDATA section of the RR are given using knowledge of the typical representation for the data.

For example, the RRs carried in a message might be shown as:

```
ISI.EDU.        MX     10 VENERA.ISI.EDU.
                MX     10 VAXA.ISI.EDU
VENERA.ISI.EDU  A      128.9.0.32
                A      10.1.0.52
VAXA.ISI.EDU    A      10.2.0.27
                A      128.9.0.33
```

The MX RRs have an RDATA section which consists of a 16-bit number followed by a domain name. The address RRs use a standard IP address format to contain a 32-bit internet address.

The above example shows six RRs, with two RRs at each of three domain names.

Similarly it may show:

```
XX.LCS.MIT.EDU. IN A      10.0.0.44
CH                 A      MIT.EDU. 2420
```

This example shows two addresses for *XX.LCS.MIT.EDU*, each of a different class.

11.1.3. Discussion of MX Records

As described above, domain servers store information as a series of resource records, each of which contains a particular piece of information about a given domain name (which is usually, but not always, a host). The simplest way to think of a RR is as a typed pair of data, a domain name matched with a relevant datum, and stored with some additional type information to help systems determine when the RR is relevant.

MX records are used to control delivery of email. The data specified in the record is a priority and a domain name. The priority controls the order in which email delivery is attempted, with the lowest number first. If two priorities are the same, a server is chosen randomly. If no servers at a given priority are responding, the mail transport agent will fall back to the next largest priority. Priority numbers do not have any absolute meaning – they are relevant only respective to other MX records for that domain name. The domain name given is the machine to which the mail will be delivered. It *must* have an associated address record (A or AAAA) – CNAME is not sufficient.

For a given domain, if there is both a CNAME record and an MX record, the MX record is in error, and will be ignored. Instead, the mail will be delivered to the server specified in the MX record pointed to by the CNAME. For example:

```
example.com.          IN  MX  10        mail.example.com.
                      IN  MX  10        mail2.example.com.
                      IN  MX  20        mail.backup.org.
mail.example.com.     IN  A   10.0.0.1
mail2.example.com.    IN  A   10.0.0.2
```

Mail delivery will be attempted to *mail.example.com* and *mail2.example.com* (in any order), and if neither of those succeed, delivery to *mail.backup.org* will be attempted.

11.1.4. Incrementing and Changing the Serial Number

Zone serial numbers are just numbers – they aren't date related. A lot of people set them to a number that represents a date, usually of the form YYYYMMDDRR (year, month, day, and number of revisions per that day). A number of people tested these numbers for Y2K compliance and set the number to the year 2000 to see if it would work. They then tried to restore the old serial number. This caused problems because serial numbers are used to indicate that a zone has been updated. If the serial number on the slave server is lower than the serial number on the master, the slave server will attempt to update its copy of the zone.

Setting the serial number to a lower number on the master server than the slave server means that the slave will not perform updates to its copy of the zone.

The solution to this is to add 2147483647 (2^31-1) to the number, reload the zone and make sure all slaves have updated to the new zone serial number, then reset the number to what you want it to be, and reload the zone again.

11.1.5. Setting TTLs

The time-to-live of the RR field is a 32-bit integer represented in units of seconds, and is primarily used by resolvers when they cache RRs. The TTL describes how long a RR can be cached before it should be discarded. The following three types of TTL are currently used in a zone file.

SOA The last field in the SOA is the negative caching TTL. This controls how long other servers will cache no-such-domain (NXDOMAIN) responses from you. The maximum time for negative caching is 3 hours (3h).

$TTL The $TTL directive at the top of the zone file (before the SOA) gives a default TTL for every RR without a specific TTL set.

RR TTLs Each RR can have a TTL as the second field in the RR, which will control how long other servers can cache the it.

All of these TTLs default to units of seconds, though units can be explicitly specified, for example, 1h30m.

11.1.6. Inverse Mapping in IPv4

Reverse name resolution (that is, translation from IP address to name) is achieved by means of the *in-addr.arpa* domain and PTR records. Entries in the in-addr.arpa domain are made in least-to-most significant order, read left to right. This is the opposite order to the way IP addresses are usually written. Thus, a machine with an IP address of 10.1.2.3 would have a corresponding *in-addr.arpa* name of *3.2.1.10.in-addr.arpa*. This name should have a PTR resource record whose data field is the name of the machine or, optionally, multiple PTR records if the machine has more than one name. For example, in the *[example.com]* domain:

```
$ORIGIN      2.1.10.in-addr.arpa
3            IN PTR foo.example.com.
```

Note: The **$ORIGIN** lines in the examples are for providing context to the examples only – they do not necessarily appear in the actual usage. They are only used here to indicate that the example is relative to the listed origin.

11.2. Load Balancing

A primitive form of load balancing can be achieved in the DNS by using multiple records (such as multiple A records) for one name.[2]

For example, if you have three WWW servers with network addresses of 10.0.0.1, 10.0.0.2 and 10.0.0.3, a set of records such as the following means that clients will connect to each machine one third of the time:

Name	TTL	CLASS	TYPE	Resource Record (RR) Data
www	600	IN	A	10.0.0.1
	600	IN	A	10.0.0.2
	600	IN	A	10.0.03

When a resolver queries for these records, BIND will rotate them and respond to the query with the records in a different order. In the example above, clients will randomly receive records in the order 1, 2, 3; 2, 3, 1; and 3, 1, 2. Most clients will use the first record returned and discard the rest.

For more detail on ordering responses, check the **rrset-order** substatement in the **options** statement covered in section 10.20.

11.3. Other Zone File Directives

The Master File Format was initially defined in RFC 1035 and has subsequently been extended. While the Master File Format itself is class independent all records in a Master File must be of the same class.

Master File Directives include **$ORIGIN**, **$INCLUDE**, and **$TTL.**

[2]Some consider this load balancing as fragile at best and completely pointless in the general case.

The $ORIGIN Directive

Syntax: **$ORIGIN** *domain-name* [*comment*]

$ORIGIN sets the domain name that will be appended to any unqualified records. When a zone is first read in there is an implicit **$ORIGIN** <zone-name>**.** The current **$ORIGIN** is appended to the domain specified in the **$ORIGIN** argument if it is not absolute.

```
$ORIGIN example.com.
WWW     CNAME   MAIN-SERVER
```

is equivalent to

```
WWW.EXAMPLE.COM. CNAME MAIN-SERVER.EXAMPLE.COM.
```

The $INCLUDE Directive

Syntax: **$INCLUDE** *filename* [*origin*] [*comment*]

Read and process the file filename as if it were included into the file at this point. If **origin** is specified the file is processed with **$ORIGIN** set to that value, otherwise the current **$ORIGIN** is used.

The origin and the current domain name revert to the values they had prior to the **$INCLUDE** once the file has been read.

> **Note:** RFC 1035 specifies that the current origin should be restored after an **$INCLUDE**, but it is silent on whether the current domain name should also be restored. BIND 9 restores both of them. This could be construed as a deviation from RFC 1035, a feature, or both.

The $TTL Directive

Syntax: **$TTL** *default-ttl* [*comment*]

Set the default Time To Live (TTL) for subsequent records with undefined TTLs. Valid TTLs are of the range 0-2147483647 seconds.

$TTL is defined in RFC 2308.

BIND Master File Extension: the $GENERATE Directive

Syntax: **$GENERATE** *range lhs* [*ttl*] [*class*] *type rhs* [*comment*]

$GENERATE is used to create a series of resource records that only differ from each other by an iterator. **$GENERATE** can be used to easily generate the sets of records required to support sub /24 reverse delegations described in RFC 2317: Classless IN-ADDR.ARPA delegation.

```
$ORIGIN 0.0.192.IN-ADDR.ARPA.
$GENERATE 1-2 0 NS SERVER$.EXAMPLE.
$GENERATE 1-127 $ CNAME $.0
```

is equivalent to

```
0.0.0.192.IN-ADDR.ARPA NS SERVER1.EXAMPLE.
0.0.0.192.IN-ADDR.ARPA. NS SERVER2.EXAMPLE.
1.0.0.192.IN-ADDR.ARPA. CNAME 1.0.0.0.192.IN-ADDR.ARPA.
2.0.0.192.IN-ADDR.ARPA. CNAME 2.0.0.0.192.IN-ADDR.ARPA.
...
127.0.0.192.IN-ADDR.ARPA. CNAME 127.0.0.0.192.IN-ADDR.ARPA.
```

range This can be one of two forms: start-stop or start-stop/step. If the first form is used, then step is set to 1. All of start, stop and step must be positive.

lhs This describes the owner name of the resource records to be created. Any single $ (dollar sign) symbols within the lhs side are replaced by the iterator value. To get a $ in the output, you need to escape the $ using a backslash \, e.g. \$. The $ may optionally be followed by modifiers which change the offset from the iterator, field width and base.

Modifiers are introduced by a { (left brace) immediately following the $ as ${offset[,width[,base]]}. For example, ${-20,3,d} subtracts 20 from the current value, prints the result as a decimal in a zero-padded field of width 3. Available output forms are decimal (d), octal (o) and hexadecimal (x or X for uppercase). The default modifier is ${0,0,d}. If the lhs is not absolute, the current $ORIGIN is appended to the name.

For compatibility with earlier versions, $$ is still recognized as indicating a literal $ in the output.

ttl Specifies the time-to-live of the generated records. If not specified this will be inherited using the normal ttl inheritance rules. class and ttl can be entered in either order.

class Specifies the class of the generated records. This must match the zone class if it is specified. class and ttl can be entered in either order.

type At present the only supported types are PTR, CNAME, DNAME, A, AAAA and NS.

rhs rhs is a domain name. It is processed similarly to lhs.

The **$GENERATE** directive is a BIND extension and not part of the standard zone file format.

BIND 8 does not support the optional TTL and CLASS fields.

11.4. Additional File Formats

In addition to the standard textual format, BIND 9 supports the ability to read or dump to zone files in other formats. The raw format is currently available as an additional format. It is a binary format representing BIND 9's internal data structure directly, thereby remarkably improving the loading time.

For a primary server, a zone file in the raw format is expected to be generated from a textual zone file by the *named-compilezone* command. (See section5.3.) For a secondary server or for a dynamic zone, it is automatically generated (if this format is specified by the **masterfile-format** option) when named dumps the zone contents after zone transfer or when applying prior updates.

If a zone file in a binary format needs manual modification, it first must be converted to a textual form by the *named-compilezone* command. All necessary modification should go to the text file, which should then be converted to the binary form by the *named-compilezone* command again.

Although the raw format uses the network byte order and avoids architecture-dependent data alignment so that it is as much portable as possible, it is primarily expected to be used inside the same single system. In order to export a zone file in the raw format or make a portable backup of the file, it is recommended to convert the file to the standard textual representation.

12. BIND 9 Security Considerations

12.1. Access Control Lists

Access Control Lists (ACLs) are address match lists that you can set up and nickname for future use in **allow-notify**, **allow-query**, **allow-query-on**, **allow-recursion**, **allow-recursion-on**, **blackhole**, **allow-transfer**, etc.

Using ACLs allows you to have finer control over who can access your name server, without cluttering up your config files with huge lists of IP addresses.

It is a good idea to use ACLs, and to control access to your server. Limiting access to your server by outside parties can help prevent spoofing and denial of service (DoS) attacks against your server.

Here is an example of how to properly apply ACLs:

```
// Set up an ACL named "bogusnets" that will block
// RFC 1918 space and some reserved space, which
// is commonly used in spoofing attacks.
acl bogusnets { 0.0.0.0/8; 1.0.0.0/8; 2.0.0.0/8;
 192.0.2.0/24; 224.0.0.0/3; 10.0.0.0/8; 172.16.0.0/12;
 192.168.0.0/16; };

// Set up an ACL called our-nets.
// Replace this with the real IP numbers.
acl our-nets { x.x.x.x/24; x.x.x.x/21; };
options {
  ...
  ...
  allow-query { our-nets; };
  allow-recursion { our-nets; };
  ...
  blackhole { bogusnets; };
  ...
};

zone "example.com" {
  type master;
  file "m/example.com";
```

```
  allow-query { any; };
};
```

This allows recursive queries of the server from the outside unless recursion has been previously disabled.

12.2. Preventing Denial of Service (DoS) attacks[1]

In 1999, a vulnerability and exploit tool were published regarding a denial of service attack based on exploiting the difference in size between a DNS query and a DNS response and the willingness of DNS servers to answer queries from any source. The vulnerability may allow remote denial of service attacks against target hosts whose IP addresses are spoofed in the DNS query. There are three parties: the target, the traffic multiplying DNS servers (amplifiers), and the attacker.

Any platform connected to the Internet may be the target of the denial of service. Service is denied by occupying all link bandwidth with responses to bogus DNS queries and potential ICMP port unreachable responses to these bogus responses. Any DNS server may be used to multiply the denial of service attack. Usually several DNS servers on networks with good bandwidth to the target are required to effectively attack the target, however the same effects can be achieved by using a larger number of amplifiers with smaller bandwidth capabilities. The attack is launched from a remote location with moderate bandwidth to the amplifiers.

Small DNS queries are sent from the attacker to each of the DNS servers. These queries contain the spoofed IP address of the target. The DNS servers respond to the small query with a large response. These responses are routed to the target, causing link congestion and possible denial of Internet connectivity.

If the number of DNS queries from the attacker is large, then the traffic may congest the DNS server's Internet link or degrade the DNS server's response time. Although no different in principle from ICMP ECHO ("ping") flooding, DNS query traffic cannot be traffic-shaped by network routers without greatly inconveniencing legitimate users.

Since this attack relies upon spoofed source IP addresses, source address checking by ISPs originating traffic is the only means to entirely defeat this form of denial of service attack.

Workaround

The tools and attacks are very straightforward and administrators can prevent their DNS servers from being used as amplifiers by configuring their servers to answer

[1] This section is derived from AUSCERT ALERT AL-1999.004. Reused by permission of AUSCERT and Glen Turner.

queries from unexpected sources with a small REFUSED response rather than a much larger name resolution response.

For the purposes of refusing queries from unexpected sources, DNS queries directed to a particular name server can be categorized into the following types. For each type of query a typical access control configuration is given. In addition, consider using controls for zone transfers. While restricting access to zone transfers is not directly related to the denial of service attack described in this alert, it may provide additional security for some sites.

These security policy examples given below are typical of a large university or ISP. It is noted where the security policy could be relaxed in a less internally hostile environment. Sites will, of course, need to modify the examples to match their own policies as appropriate.

The examples in this section use a fictitious company with the domain name *example.com* and the fictitious IP address range 126.0.0.0/8.

When configuring a particular name server, first set the default level of query and zone transfer access. Then override this with specific access controls for each zone, according to its type (either (2) primary, (3) official secondary or (4) stealth secondary).

(1) Queries for Any Name

Allow queries from "trusted" sources only. Trusted sources are defined as hosts for which the DNS server provides recursive DNS name resolution. These hosts would usually lie within an ISP's or enterprise's network. These hosts usually have the DNS server listed in a configuration file such as */etc/resolv.conf* or supplied to it in a PPP, DHCP or BOOTP response. Allow no zone transfers.

The default case is handled by setting the BIND options.

This is an extract from the */etc/named.conf* file on all of *example.com*'s BIND DNS servers.

```
// DNS clients at example.com
acl "trusted" {
        localhost;
        126.0.0.0/8;     // Hosts at example.com
};

// Known fake source addresses shouldn't be replied to.
// For external queries, these should be blocked by
// example.com's border router.
acl "bogon" {
         0.0.0.0/8;      // Null address
         1.0.0.0/8;      // IANA reserved, popular fakes
         2.0.0.0/8;
```

```
          192.0.2.0/24;   // Test address
          224.0.0.0/3;    // Multicast addresses
          // Enterprise networks may or may not be
          // bogus.
          10.0.0.0/8;
          172.16.0.0/12;
          192.168.0.0/16;
};

options {
        directory "/var/named";
        allow-query {
                trusted;
        };
        allow-transfer {
                none;
        };
        blackhole {
                bogon;
        };
};

// Bootstrap the root.
// This is an example for overriding the defaults.
zone "." {
        type hint;
        file "named.ca";
};

// 127.0.0.0/24  The loopback network.
zone "0.0.127.in-addr.arpa" {
        type master;
        file "127.in-addr.arpa";
        allow-query {
                trusted;
        };
        // Every DNS server should be a
        // master for 127.0.0.0/24.
        allow-transfer {
                none;
        };
};
```

(2) Queries for Names in Primary Zones

A "primary zone" is a zone for which a server has the DNS master file described in RFC 1035 and the server is one of the name servers that has been delegated the domain.

Allow queries from all sources. Allow zone transfers from official and stealth secondaries.

dns0.example.com is the primary DNS server for the zone "*example.com*".

This is an extract from the */etc/named.conf* file on *dns0.example.com*. The extract defines the zone "*example.com*" and lists the zone's secondary DNS servers.

```
// Official and stealth secondaries.
acl "example-xfer" {
        126.0.2.2;        // dns1.example.com (official)
        126.0.1.1;        // dns2.example.com (official)
        126.0.3.4;        // mailhub.example.com (stealth)
};

zone "example.com" {
        type master;      // official
        file "primary/example.com";
        allow-query {
                any;
        };
        allow-transfer {
                localhost;
                example-xfer;
        };
};

// 126.0.0.0/8
zone "0.126.in-addr.arpa" {
        type master;      // official
        file "primary/0.126.in-addr.arpa";
        allow-query {
                any;
        };
        allow-transfer {
                localhost;
                example-xfer;
        };
};
```

As noted above, any sub-domains of *example.com* present on this DNS server must allow queries from any source, as the parent domain on this server allows queries from any source.

(3) Queries for Names in Official Secondary Zones

An "official secondary zone" is a zone for which the server has a zone transfer of the DNS master file and is one of the name servers that has been delegated the domain. Official secondary zones exist to add robustness to the Domain Name System.

Allow queries from all sources. Possibly allow zone transfers from official and stealth secondaries.

dns1.example.com is an official secondary DNS server for the zone *"example.com"*.

This is an extract from the */etc/named.conf* file on *dns1.example.com.* The extract defines the zone *"example.com"*.

```
// Official and stealth secondaries.
acl "example-xfer" {
        126.0.2.2;      // dns1.example.com (official)
        126.0.1.1;      // dns2.example.com (official)
        126.0.3.4;      // mailhub.example.com (stealth)
};

zone "example.com" {
        type slave;             // official
        file "secondary/example.com";
        masters {
                126.0.2.1;    // dns0.example.com
        };
        allow-query {
                any;
        };
        allow-transfer {
                localhost;
                example-xfer;
        };
};

// 126.0.0.0/8
zone "0.126.in-addr.arpa" {
        type slave;             // official
        file "secondary/0.126.in-addr.arpa";
        masters {
                126.0.2.1;    // dns0.example.com
        };
        allow-query {
                any;
        };
        allow-transfer {
```

```
                localhost;
                example-xfer;
        };
};
```

As noted above, any sub-domains of "*example.com*" present on this DNS server must allow queries from any source, as the parent domain on this server allows queries from any source.

(4) Queries for Names in Stealth Secondary Zones

A "stealth secondary zone" is a zone for which the server has a zone transfer of the DNS master file but is not one of the name servers that has been delegated the domain. Stealth secondary zones are often used to add performance to DNS resolution, especially at sites reachable only across slow wide-area network links or on machines containing DNS-intensive applications such as e-mail.

Allow queries from "trusted" sources only. Allow no zone transfers.

It may be administratively convenient to allow queries from all sources, as this minimizes the risk of outages if official secondary zones and stealth secondary zones are confused or if all the users of the stealth secondary zone are not known. If queries are limited to "trusted" sources only, then a careful eye should be kept on the DNS server log.

mailhub.example.com is a stealth secondary DNS server for the zone "*example.com*".

This is an extract from the */etc/named.conf* file on *mailhub.example.com*. The extract defines the zone "*example.com*".

```
acl "trusted" {
        localhost;
        126.0.0.0/8;     // Hosts at example.com
};

// Official and stealth secondaries.
acl "example-xfer" {
        126.0.2.2;        // dns1.example.com (official)
        126.0.1.1;        // dns2.example.com (official)
        126.0.3.4;        // mailhub.example.com (stealth)
};

zone "example.com" {
        type slave;            // stealth
        file "secondary/example.com";
        masters {
```

```
                126.0.2.1;      // dns0.example.com
        };
        allow-query {
                trusted;
                // or "any;" if you don't have good records
                // of the expected users of the stealth
                // secondary.
        };
        allow-transfer {
                localhost;
                example-xfer;
        };
};

// 126.0.0.0/8
zone "0.126.in-addr.arpa" {
        type slave;             // stealth
        file "secondary/0.126.in-addr.arpa";
        masters {
                126.0.2.1;      // dns0.example.com
        };
        allow-query {
                trusted;
                // or "any;" if you don't have good records
                // of the expected users of the stealth
                // secondary.
        };
        allow-transfer {
                localhost;
                example-xfer;
        };
};
```

As noted above, any sub-domains of *example.com* present o this DNS server must allow queries from at least the hosts in the "trusted" access control list, as the parent domain on this server allows queries from that list.

An exception to the guidelines in (2) to (4) above is that within the configuration of each DNS server, a sub-domain cannot service a smaller range of query sources than its parent domain. If a DNS server allows queries from any source for the domain *example.com*, then it must also allow queries from any source for the delegated sub-domain *instructive.example.com*.

It is administratively useful to allow DNS zone transfers between all primary and secondary DNS servers. This eases the debugging of zone transfer faults.

Similarly, allowing DNS zone transfers to a limited number of hosts used by network administrators may also be convenient. Allowing zone transfers to all "trusted" users may be too trusting in environments such as Internet service providers or universities.

"Stealth primary zones" also exist. As these are mainly used inside firewalled environments, it is not useful to describe their configuration in this document

There are obvious limitations to these workarounds. As stated previously, the only solution to this problem currently is that all sites implement source address checking to prevent packets with spoofed IP addresses leaving their networks. Nonetheless, these suggestions will assist in mitigating current forms of the attack and may provide some additional security.

12.3. Limiting Version Number Availability

By default, the BIND version number (and hostname) can be read using a DNS query utility such as *dig*:

```
dig @dns0.example.com version.bind chaos txt
```

Or for example:

```
# host -c chaos -t txt version.bind
version.bind descriptive text "9.4.1-P1"
```

This query may be restricted by:

- **allow-query** option
- **version** option
- or by defining a custom *bind* zone in the **CHAOS** class.

Allowing the version number of any software to be known to everyone is usually undesirable. Access to the version number can be restricted to local users by adding the following to */etc/named.conf* on all BIND DNS servers. (Restricting the version or defining a different version details for requests can be done using the **version** option introduced on page 124.)

Note: this **CHAOS** zone needs to be done within a **view** of class **CHAOS**.

```
// Control access to BIND version number to
// users at example.com only.
zone "bind" chaos {
        type master;
```

```
        file "primary/bind";
        allow-query {
                trusted;²
        };
        allow-transfer {
                none;
        };
};
```

And by also adding the file */var/named/primary/bind* containing only:

```
; File /var/named/primary/bind
$ORIGIN bind.
@       1D CHAOS SOA    localhost. root.localhost. (
                        1               ; serial
                        3H              ; refresh
                        1H              ; retry
                        1W              ; expiry
                        1D )            ; minimum
           CHAOS NS     localhost.
; EOF
```

Note: The zone file could also define a TXT record for the "*version*" and/or "*hostname*". BIND 9 also has **version** and **hostname** options; see page 124 for details.

12.4. Controlling Log Messages

When being used to vector an attack, the BIND DNS server can generate a large number of log messages of the form:

```
unapproved query from [99.2.3.4].12345 for "example.net"
```

The BIND DNS server can be configured to log these messages to a separate file, a separate syslog facility (allowing logging on a remote machine) or to discard all security messages.

Unfortunately, discarding security messages also discards messages referring to users of stealth zones that have been accidently denied access and messages generated by the confusion of an official secondary zone with a stealth secondary zone. It would be wise to review the log messages for these events before considering disabling security event logging.

[2] The "trusted" ACL was defined earlier; see page 163.

12.5. Controlling Visibility of DNS Servers

Not all DNS servers are known to ISPs or the network administrators of large enterprises. In particular, there is no simple means of determining the presence of caching-only DNS servers on hosts. These servers are usually not configured to regulate the source of DNS queries.

As a result, these servers can be used to amplify DNS-based denial of service attacks even if all the DNS servers owned by the ISP regulate the source of DNS queries.

Organizations should consider limiting DNS UDP and TCP access to just the known DNS servers by configuring access restrictions on their network's border router.

These access restrictions can be summarized as:

Servers containing primary or official secondary zones:

Remote *:* <–> address:53 Local (UDP/TCP)

Each DNS server that acts as a resolver (that is, is listed in *\/etc/resolv.conf* or supplied by PPP, DHCP or BOOTP):

Remote *:53 <–> address:* Local (UDP/TCP)

Or, if the DNS servers are configured with "query-source * port 53;":

Remote *:53 <–> address:53 Local (UDP)

Remote *:53 <–> address:* Local (TCP)

Servers containing unofficial secondary zones have varying requirements, depending on the location of the primary zone server:

Remote master:* <–> address:53 Local (UDP) (Notify)

Remote master:53 <–> address:* Local (UDP) (SOA query)

Remote master:53 <–> address:* Local (TCP) (IXFR)

Or, if the DNS servers are configured with "query-source * port 53;":

Remote master:* <–> address:53 Local (UDP) (Notify)

Remote master:53 <–> address:53 Local (UDP) (SOA query)

Remote master:53 <–> address:* Local (TCP) (IXFR)

There are two traps for access list authors: Any DNS UDP request may be given as a DNS TCP request; and the DNS NOTIFY command must be allowed for servers of primary zones to inform servers of secondary zones of a change in the master file.

Implementing these access restrictions prevents queries from hosts inside the network and denies direct access from hosts inside the network to external name servers.

Denying direct access is unlikely to affect most hosts: these make a recursive query to a pre-configured DNS server.

Denying direct access to external name servers is likely to break caching-only DNS name servers on hosts. These servers can be reconfigured to forward DNS requests to one or more of the DNS servers that has DNS visibility to the Internet. A caching-only name server configuration is presented in Appendix D.

12.6. Chroot and Setuid

On UNIX servers, it is possible to run BIND in a *chrooted* environment (using the chroot() function) by specifying the "-t" option for *named*. This can help improve system security by placing BIND in a "sandbox", which will limit the damage done if a server is compromised.

Another useful feature in the UNIX version of BIND is the ability to run the daemon as an unprivileged user (-u *user*). Running as an unprivileged user when using the chroot feature is suggested.

Here is an example command line to load BIND in a chroot sandbox, */var/named*, and to run *named* setuid to user 202:

```
/usr/local/sbin/named -u 202 -t /var/named
```

The chroot Environment

In order for a *chroot* environment to work properly in a particular directory (for example, */var/named*), you will need to set up an environment that includes everything BIND needs to run. From BIND's point of view, */var/named* is the root of the filesystem. You will need to adjust the values of options like like **directory** and **pid-file** to account for this.

Unlike with earlier versions of BIND, you typically will not need to compile *named* statically nor install shared libraries under the new root. However, depending on your operating system, you may need to set up things like */dev/zero*, */dev/random*, */dev/log*, and */etc/localtime*.

Using the setuid Function

Prior to running the *named* daemon, use the *touch* utility (to change file access and modification times) or the *chown* utility (to set the user id and/or group id) on files to which you want BIND to write. Note that if the *named* daemon is running as an unprivileged user, it will not be able to bind to new restricted ports if the server is reloaded.

12.7. Dynamic Update Security

Access to the dynamic update facility should be strictly limited. In earlier versions of BIND, the only way to do this was based on the IP address of the host requesting the update, by listing an IP address or network prefix in the **allow-update** zone option. This method is insecure since the source address of the update UDP packet is easily forged. Also note that if the IP addresses allowed by the **allow-update** option include the address of a slave server which performs forwarding of dynamic updates, the master can be trivially attacked by sending the update to the slave, which will forward it to the master with its own source IP address causing the master to approve it without question.

For these reasons, it is strongly recommended that updates be cryptographically authenticated by means of transaction signatures (TSIG). That is, the **allow-update** option should list only TSIG key names, not IP addresses or network prefixes. Alternatively, the new **update-policy** option can be used.

Some sites choose to keep all dynamically-updated DNS data in a subdomain and delegate that subdomain to a separate zone. This way, the top-level zone containing critical data such as the IP addresses of public web and mail servers need not allow dynamic update at all.

13. Troubleshooting

13.1. How can I figure out what's wrong?

The best solution to solving installation and configuration issues is to take preventative measures by setting up logging files beforehand. The log files provide a source of hints and information that can be used to figure out what went wrong and how to fix the problem. Configurations for logging and debugging are covered in section 10.5.

13.2. Where Can I Get Help?

The Internet Systems Consortium (ISC) offers a wide range of support and service agreements for BIND and DHCP servers. Four levels of premium support are available and each level includes support for all ISC programs, significant discounts on products and training, and a recognized priority on bug fixes and non-funded feature requests. In addition, ISC offers a standard support agreement package which includes services ranging from bug fix announcements to remote support. It also includes training in BIND and DHCP.

To discuss arrangements for commercial support, contact info@isc.org or visit the ISC web page at http://www.isc.org/services/support/.

An open community for BIND discussion and free support is available via the BIND Users mailing list. Archives can be found via http://www.isc.org/ops/lists/.

To join, send an email to bind-users-request@isc.org or visit the website above.

A. A Brief History of the DNS and BIND

Although the "official" beginning of the Domain Name System occurred in 1984 with the publication of RFC 920, the core of the new system was described in 1983 in RFCs 882 and 883. From 1984 to 1987, the ARPAnet (the precursor to today's Internet) became a testbed of experimentation for developing the new naming/addressing scheme in a rapidly expanding, operational network environment. New RFCs were written and published in 1987 that modified the original documents to incorporate improvements based on the working model. RFC 1034, "Domain Names-Concepts and Facilities", and RFC 1035, "Domain Names-Implementation and Specification" were published and became the standards upon which all DNS implementations are built.

The first working domain name server, called "Jeeves", was written in 1983-84 by Paul Mockapetris for operation on DEC Tops-20 machines located at the University of Southern California's Information Sciences Institute (USC-ISI) and SRI International's Network Information Center (SRI-NIC). A DNS server for Unix machines, the Berkeley Internet Name Domain (BIND) package, was written soon after by a group of graduate students at the University of California at Berkeley under a grant from the US Defense Advanced Research Projects Administration (DARPA).

Versions of BIND through 4.8.3 were maintained by the Computer Systems Research Group (CSRG) at UC Berkeley. Douglas Terry, Mark Painter, David Riggle and Songnian Zhou made up the initial BIND project team. After that, additional work on the software package was done by Ralph Campbell. Kevin Dunlap, a Digital Equipment Corporation employee on loan to the CSRG, worked on BIND for 2 years, from 1985 to 1987. Many other people also contributed to BIND development during that time: Doug Kingston, Craig Partridge, Smoot Carl-Mitchell, Mike Muuss, Jim Bloom and Mike Schwartz. BIND maintenance was subsequently handled by Mike Karels and Øivind Kure.

BIND versions 4.9 and 4.9.1 were released by Digital Equipment Corporation (now Compaq Computer Corporation). Paul Vixie, then a DEC employee, became BIND's primary caretaker. He was assisted by Phil Almquist, Robert Elz, Alan Barrett, Paul Albitz, Bryan Beecher, Andrew Partan, Andy Cherenson, Tom Limoncelli, Berthold Paffrath, Fuat Baran, Anant Kumar, Art Harkin, Win Treese, Don Lewis, Christophe Wolfhugel, and others.

In 1994, BIND version 4.9.2 was sponsored by Vixie Enterprises. Paul Vixie became BIND's principal architect/programmer.

BIND versions from 4.9.3 onward have been developed and maintained by the Internet Systems Consortium and its predecessor, the Internet Software Consortium, with support being provided by ISC's sponsors.

As co-architects/programmers, Bob Halley and Paul Vixie released the first production-ready version of BIND version 8 in May 1997.

BIND version 9 was released in September 2000 and is a major rewrite of nearly all aspects of the underlying BIND architecture.

BIND versions 4 and 8 are officially deprecated. No additional development is done on BIND version 4 or BIND version 8.

BIND development work is made possible today by the sponsorship of several corporations, and by the tireless work efforts of numerous individuals.

B. BIND 8 to BIND 9 Migration Notes

This appendix provides information about differences between BIND 8 and BIND 9. BIND 9 is designed to be mostly upwards compatible with BIND 8, but there are still a number of caveats you should be aware of when upgrading an existing BIND 8 installation to use BIND 9.[1]

B.1. Configuration File Compatibility

B.1.1. Unimplemented Options and Changed Defaults

The BIND 9 name server supports most, but not all, of the configuration options of the BIND 8 name server. For a complete list of implemented options, see chapter 10.

If your *named.conf* file uses an unimplemented option, the BIND 9 name server will log a warning message. A message is also logged about each option whose default has changed unless the option is set explicitly in *named.conf*.

The default of the **transfer-format** option has changed from **one-answer** to **many-answers**. If you have slave servers that do not understand the **many-answers** zone transfer format (e.g., BIND 4.9.5 and older) you need to explicitly specify "**transfer-format one-answer;**" in either the **options** block or a **server** statement. (See page 114 for details.)

B.1.2. Handling of Configuration File Errors

In BIND 9, *named* refuses to start if it detects an error in *named.conf*. Earlier versions would start despite errors, causing the server to run with a partial configuration. Errors detected during subsequent reloads do not cause the server to exit.

Errors in master files do not cause the server to exit, but they do cause the zone not to load.

[1] This appendix is mostly from the "migration" file included with the BIND source code plus some additions from SUN.

B.1.3. Logging

The set of logging categories in BIND 9 is different from that in BIND 8. If you have customized your logging on a per-category basis, you need to modify your **logging** statement to use the new categories.

Another difference is that the **logging** statement only takes effect after the entire *named.conf* file has been read. This means that when the server starts up, any messages about errors in the configuration file are always logged to the default destination (syslog) when the server first starts up, regardless of the contents of the **logging** statement. In BIND 8, the new logging configuration took effect immediately after the **logging** statement was read.

B.1.4. Notify Messages and Refresh Queries

The source address and port for Notify messages and Refresh queries is now controlled by **notify-source** and **transfer-source**, respectively, rather than **query-source** as in BIND 8. For more details, see page 116.

B.1.5. Multiple Classes

Multiple classes have to be put into explicit views for each class.

B.2. Zone File Compatibility

B.2.1. Strict RFC1035 Interpretation of TTLs in Zone Files

BIND 9 strictly complies with the RFC 1035 and RFC 2308 rules regarding omitted time-to-live (TTL) entries in zone files. Omitted TTLs are replaced by the value specified with the **$TTL** directive, or by the previous explicit TTL if there is no **$TTL** directive.

If there is no **$TTL** directive and the first Resource Record (RR) in the file does not have an explicit TTL field, the zone file is illegal according to RFC 1035 since the TTL of the first RR is undefined. Unfortunately, BIND 4 and many versions of BIND 8 accept such files without warning and use the value of the SOA MINTTL field as a default for missing TTL values.

BIND 9.0 and 9.1 completely refused to load such files. BIND 9.2 and newer emulate the nonstandard BIND 4/8 SOA MINTTL behavior and load the files anyway (provided the SOA is the first record in the file), but will issue the warning message “no TTL specified; using SOA MINTTL instead”.

To avoid problems, we recommend that you use a **$TTL** directive in each zone file.

B.2.2. Periods in SOA Serial Numbers Deprecated

Some versions of BIND allow SOA serial numbers with an embedded period, like "3.002", and convert them into integers in a rather unintuitive way. This feature is not supported by BIND 9; serial numbers must be integers.

B.2.3. Handling of Unbalanced Quotes

TXT records with unbalanced quotes, like 'host TXT "foo', were not treated as errors in some versions of BIND. If your zone files contain such records, you will get potentially confusing error messages like "unexpected end of file" because BIND 9 will interpret everything up to the next quote character as a literal string.

B.2.4. Handling of Line Breaks

Some versions of BIND accept RRs containing line breaks that are not properly quoted with parentheses, like the following SOA:

```
@       IN SOA  ns.example. hostmaster.example.
                ( 1 3600 1800 1814400 3600 )
```

This is not legal master file syntax and will be treated as an error by BIND 9. The fix is to move the opening parenthesis to the first line.

B.2.5. Unimplemented BIND 8 Extensions

$GENERATE: The "$$" construct for getting a literal $ (dollar sign) into a domain name is deprecated. Use \$ instead.

B.2.6. TXT records are no longer automatically split.

Some versions of BIND accepted strings TXT RDATA that contained more than 255 characters and silently split them in to multiple RDATA records to comply with protocol. This feature has been removed, and the following error is produced upon reading these records:

```
dns_rdata_fromtext: local.db:119: ran out of space
```

To address, split the string in the zone data file at or before the 255 character in to two or more TXT records.

B.3. Interoperability Impact of New Protocol Features

B.3.1. EDNS0

BIND 9 uses EDNS0 (RFC 2671) to advertise its receive buffer size. It also sets DO EDNS flag bit in queries to indicate that it wishes to receive DNSSEC responses.

Most older servers that do not support EDNS0, including prior versions of BIND, will send a FORMERR or NOTIMP response to these queries. When this happens, BIND 9 will automatically retry the query without EDNS0.

Unfortunately, there exists at least one non-BIND name server implementation that silently ignores these queries instead of sending an error response. Resolving names in zones where all or most authoritative servers use this server will be very slow or fail completely. The manufacturer of the name server is working on a solution.

When BIND 9 communicates with a server that does support EDNS0, such as another BIND 9 server, responses of up to 4096 bytes may be transmitted as a single UDP datagram which is subject to fragmentation at the IP level. If a firewall incorrectly drops IP fragments, it can cause resolution to slow down dramatically or fail.

B.3.2. Zone Transfers

Outgoing zone transfers now use the **many-answers** format by default. This format is not understood by certain old versions of BIND 4. You can work around this problem using the option "**transfer-format one-answer;**", but since these old versions all have known security problems, the correct fix is to upgrade the slave servers.

Zone transfers to Windows 2000 DNS servers sometimes fail due to a bug in the Windows 2000 DNS server where DNS messages larger than 16K are not handled properly. Obtain the latest service pack for Windows 2000 from Microsoft to address this issue. In the meantime, the problem can be worked around by setting "**transfer-format one-answer;**". More details are at Microsoft's website at http://support.microsoft.com/default.aspx?scid=kb;en-us;297936.

B.4. Unrestricted Character Set

BIND 9 does not restrict the character set of domain names; it is fully 8-bit clean in accordance with RFC 2181 section 11.

It is strongly recommended that hostnames published in the DNS follow the RFC 952 rules, but BIND 9.2 and above will not enforce this restriction.

Historically, some applications have suffered from security flaws where data originating from the network, such as names returned by gethostbyaddr(), are used with insufficient checking and may cause a breach of security when containing unexpected characters; see http://www.cert.org/advisories/CA-1996-04.html for details.

Some earlier versions of BIND attempt to protect these flawed applications from attack by discarding data containing characters deemed inappropriate in host names or mail addresses, under the control of the **check-names** option in *named.conf* and/or "**options no-check-names**" in *resolv.conf*[2]. BIND 9.2 provided no such protection; advice was that applications with these flaws should be upgraded.

BIND 9.3 onwards implements **check-names**. See page 107 about the **check-names** option for more details.

B.5. Server Administration Tools

B.5.1. ndc Replaced by rndc

The *ndc* program has been replaced by *rndc*, which is capable of remote operation. Unlike *ndc*, *rndc* requires a configuration file. The easiest way to generate a configuration file is to run "`rndc-confgen -a`"; see sections 4.3 and 4.5 for details.

The BIND 8 *ndc* and BIND 9 *rndc* name server control tools are not backward compatible: *rndc* can't talk to the BIND 8 name server and *ndc* can't talk to the BIND 9 name server. Features, options, default modes of operation, and configuration file requirements have changed.

In BIND 9, *rndc* uses an authenticated TCP/IP inet control channel, by default and is not backward compatible with BIND 8 (which uses UNIX domain socket by default).

When using *rndc*, you need to specify a **key** clause to communicate with the name server. It is mandatory that the BIND 9 server and the *rndc* client share the same key. Using the BIND 8 controls entry in BIND 9 will result in an error message.

Some command options have changed from the *ndc* to the *rndc* implementation. This includes the "-c" option, which has a different syntax in BIND 9. Therefore, to specify the control channel in BIND 9, use:

```
rndc -s server -p port
```

B.5.2. nsupdate Differences

The BIND 8 implementation of *nsupdate* had an undocumented feature where an update request would be broken down into multiple requests based upon the discovered zones that contained the records. This behavior has not been implemented in BIND 9. Each update request must pertain to a single zone, but it is still possible to do multiple

[2]Some *resolv.conf* formats don't support this.

updates in a single invocation of *nsupdate* by terminating each update with an empty line or a "send" command.

In BIND 9.2 and above, the syntax of the "-k" option changes in *nsupdate*. Instead of "-k keydir::keyname" the syntax is now "-k keyfile". The only other difference is that whereas a blank line was used to signal sending the input to the server, an explicit "send" sub-command is now used to do the same. See section 5.4 for further details.

B.5.3. named Differences

In the BIND 9 *named* server, the "-g *group_name*", "-q", "-r" and "-w *directory*" options are not supported, and "-c *config_file*" replaces the BIND 8.x "-b *config_file*". See section 4.1 for further details.

In BIND 9.3 and later, *named* no longer provides the following functionality:

- Inverse IPv6 queries to the obsolete *ip6.int* domain. The *ip6.arpa* domain is obsoleted by the *ip6.int* domain. See RFC 3596. (Also see page 68 for more details.)
- IPv6 does not forward A6 lookups, deprecated by RFC 3363.
- IPv6 "bitstring" not supported, primary will refuse to load zone files with binary labels. Deprecated by RFC 3363.
- Zones containing MD (Mail Destination) and MF (Mail Forwarder) will now be rejected. The MD and MF resource record (RR) types were originally introduced in RFC 882 and subsequently obsoleted in RFC 1035 by the MX RR. See section 11.1.3 for information about MX records.

B.6. No Information Leakage Between Zones

BIND 9 stores the authoritative data for each zone in a separate data structure, as recommended in RFC 1035 and as required by DNSSEC and IXFR. When a BIND 9 server is authoritative for both a child zone and its parent, it will have two distinct sets of NS records at the delegation point: the authoritative NS records at the child's apex, and a set of glue NS records in the parent.

BIND 8 was unable to properly distinguish between these two sets of NS records and would "leak" the child's NS records into the parent, effectively causing the parent zone to be silently modified: responses and zone transfers from the parent contained the child's NS records rather than the glue configured into the parent (if any). In the case of children of type "stub", this behavior was documented as a feature, allowing the glue NS records to be omitted from the parent configuration.

Sites that were relying on this BIND 8 behavior need to add any omitted glue NS records, and any necessary glue A records, to the parent zone.

Although stub zones can no longer be used as a mechanism for injecting NS records into their parent zones, they are still useful as a way of directing queries for a given domain to a particular set of name servers.

B.7. Umask Not Modified

The BIND 8 *named* unconditionally sets the umask to 022. BIND 9 does not; the umask inherited from the parent process remains in effect. This may cause files created by *named*, such as journal files, to be created with different file permissions than they did in BIND 8. If necessary, the umask should be set explicitly in the script used to start the *named* process.

C. Request for Comments (RFCs)

Specification documents for the Internet protocol suite, including the DNS, are published as part of the Request for Comments (RFCs) series of technical notes. The standards themselves are defined by the Internet Engineering Task Force (IETF) and the Internet Engineering Steering Group (IESG). RFCs can be obtained online via FTP at ftp://www.isi.edu/in-notes/RFC*xxxx*.txt (where *xxxx* is the number of the RFC). RFCs are also available via the Web at http://www.ietf.org/rfc/.

Standards

RFC 974 C. Partridge, *Mail Routing and the Domain System*, January 1986.

RFC 1034 P.V. Mockapetris, *Domain Names – Concepts and Facilities*, November 1987.

RFC 1035 P. V. Mockapetris, *Domain Names – Implementation and Specification*, November 1987.

Proposed Standards

RFC 2181 R., R. Bush Elz, *Clarifications to the DNS Specification*, July 1997.

RFC 2308 M. Andrews, *Negative Caching of DNS Queries*, March 1998.

RFC 1995 M. Ohta, *Incremental Zone Transfer in DNS*, August 1996.

RFC 1996 P. Vixie, *A Mechanism for Prompt Notification of Zone Changes*, August 1996.

RFC 2136 P. Vixie, S. Thomson, Y. Rekhter, and J. Bound, *Dynamic Updates in the Domain Name System*, April 1997.

RFC 2671 P. Vixie, *Extension Mechanisms for DNS (EDNS0)*, August 1997.

RFC 2672 M. Crawford, *Non-Terminal DNS Name Redirection*, August 1999.

RFC 2845 P. Vixie, O. Gudmundsson, D. Eastlake, 3rd, and B. Wellington, *Secret Key Transaction Authentication for DNS (TSIG)*, May 2000.

RFC 2930 D. Eastlake, 3rd, *Secret Key Establishment for DNS (TKEY RR)*, September 2000.

RFC 2931 D. Eastlake, 3rd, *DNS Request and Transaction Signatures (SIG(0)s)*, September 2000.

RFC 3007 B. Wellington, Secure Domain Name System (DNS) Dynamic Update, November 2000.

RFC 3645 S. Kwan, P. Garg, J. Gilroy, L. Esibov, J. Westhead, R. Hall, Generic Security Service Algorithm for Secret Key Transaction Authentication for DNS (GSS-TSIG), October 2003.

DNS Security Proposed Standards

RFC 3225 D. Conrad, *Indicating Resolver Support of DNSSEC*, December 2001.

RFC 3833 D. Atkins, R. Austein, *Threat Analysis of the Domain Name System (DNS)*, August 2004.

RFC 4033 R. Arends, R. Austein, M. Larson, D. Massey, S. Rose, *DNS Security Introduction and Requirements*, March 2005.

RFC 4044 R. Arends, R. Austein, M. Larson, D. Massey, S. Rose, *Resource Records for the DNS Security Extensions*, March 2005.

RFC 4035 R. Arends, R. Austein, M. Larson, D. Massey, S. Rose, *Protocol Modifications for the DNS Security Extensions*, March 2005.

Obsoleted DNS Security RFCs

Most of these have been consolidated into RFC 4033, RFC 4034 and RFC 4035 which collectively describe DNSSECbis.

RFC 2065 D. Eastlake, 3rd and C. Kaufman, *Domain Name System Security Extensions*, January 1997.

RFC 2137 D. Eastlake, 3rd, *Secure Domain Name System Dynamic Update*, April 1997.

RFC 2535 Eastlake 3rd D., *Domain Name System Security Extensions*, March, 1999.

RFC 3008 Wellington B., *Domain Name System Security (DNSSEC) Signing Authority*, November 2000.

RFC 3090 Lewis E., *DNS Security Extension Clarification on Zone Status*, March 2001.

RFC 3445 Massey D., Rose S., *Limiting the Scope of the KEY Resource Record (RR)*, December 2002 .

RFC 3655 Wellington B., Gudmundsson O., *Redefinition of DNS Authenticated Data (AD) bit*, November 2003.

RFC 3658 Gudmundsson O., *Delegation Signer (DS) Resource Record (RR)*, December 2003.

RFC 3755 Weiler S., *Legacy Resolver Compatibility for Delegation Signer (DS)*, May 2004.

RFC 3757 Kolkman O., Schlyter J., Lewis E., *Domain Name System KEY (DNSKEY) Resource Record (RR) Secure Entry Point (SEP) Flag*, April 2004.

RFC 3845 Schlyter J., *DNS Security (DNSSEC) NextSECure (NSEC) RDATA Format*, August 2004.

Proposed Standards Still Under Development

RFC 1886 S. Thomson and C. Huitema, *DNS Extensions to support IP version 6*, December 1995.

Other Important RFCs About DNS Implementation

RFC 1535 E. Gavron, *A Security Problem and Proposed Correction With Widely Deployed DNS Software.*, October 1993.

RFC 1536 A. Kumar, J. Postel, C. Neuman, P. Danzig, and S. Miller, *Common DNS Implementation Errors and Suggested Fixes*, October 1993.

RFC 1982 R. Elz and R. Bush, *Serial Number Arithmetic*, August 1996.

Resource Record Types

RFC 1183 C.F. Everhart, L. A. Mamakos, R. Ullmann, and P. Mockapetris, *New DNS RR Definitions*, October 1990.

RFC 1706 B. Manning and R. Colella, *DNS NSAP Resource Records*, October 1994.

RFC 2168 R. Daniel and M. Mealling, *Resolution of Uniform Resource Identifiers using the Domain Name System*, June 1997.

RFC 1876 C. Davis, P. Vixie, T., and I. Dickinson, *A Means for Expressing Location Information in the Domain Name System*, January 1996.

RFC 2052 A. Gulbrandsen and P. Vixie, *A DNS RR for Specifying the Location of Services.*, October 1996.

RFC 2163 A. Allocchio, *Using the Internet DNS to Distribute MIXER Conformant Global Address Mapping*, January 1998.

RFC 2230 R. Atkinson, *Key Exchange Delegation Record for the DNS*, October 1997.

Obsolete and Unimplemented Experimental RRs

RFC 1712 C. Farrell, M. Schulze, S. Pleitner, and D. Baldoni, *DNS Encoding of Geographical Location*, November 1994.

DNS and the Internet

RFC 1101 P. V. Mockapetris, *DNS Encoding of Network Names and Other Types*, April 1989.

RFC 1123 Braden, *Requirements for Internet Hosts - Application and Support*, October 1989.

RFC 1591 J. Postel, *Domain Name System Structure and Delegation*, March 1994.

RFC 2317 H. Eidnes, G. de Groot, and P. Vixie, *Classless IN-ADDR.ARPA Delegation*, March 1998.

DNS Operations

RFC 1537 P. Beertema, *Common DNS Data File Configuration Errors*, October 1993.

RFC 1912 D. Barr, *Common DNS Operational and Configuration Errors*, February 1996.

RFC 2010 B. Manning and P. Vixie, *Operational Criteria for Root Name Servers.*, October 1996.

RFC 2219 M. Hamilton and R. Wright, *Use of DNS Aliases for Network Services.*, October 1997.

Other DNS-related RFCs

RFC 1464 R. Rosenbaum, *Using the Domain Name System To Store Arbitrary String Attributes*, May 1993.

RFC 1713 A. Romao, *Tools for DNS Debugging*, November 1994.

RFC 1794 T. Brisco, *DNS Support for Load Balancing*, April 1995.

RFC 2240 O. Vaughan, *A Legal Basis for Domain Name Allocation*, November 1997.

RFC 2345 J. Klensin, T. Wolf, and G. Oglesby, *Domain Names and Company Name Retrieval*, May 1998.

RFC 2352 O. Vaughan, *A Convention For Using Legal Names as Domain Names*, May 1998.

Internet Drafts

Internet Drafts (IDs) are rough-draft working documents of the Internet Engineering Task Force. They are, in essence, RFCs in the preliminary stages of development. Implementors are cautioned not to regard IDs as archival, and they should not be quoted or cited in any formal documents unless accompanied by the disclaimer that they are "works in progress." IDs have a lifespan of six months after which they are deleted unless updated by their authors.

D. Example caching-only name server configuration

A configuration extract for a caching-only name server designed to service only the host it is running on is given below.

Extracts from the */etc/named.conf* file:

```
options {
    // no version
    version none;
    // "only" misleads -- if all the forwarders fail we
    // are no worse off than with only a /etc/resolv.conf,
    // but we get the benefit of DNS name caching in the
    // meantime.
    forward only;
    forwarders {
            // From previous "nameserver" entries in
            // /etc/resolv.conf.
            126.0.2.1;     // dns0.example.com
            126.0.2.2;     // dns1.example.com
            126.0.1.1;     // dns2.example.com
    };
    allow-query {
           localhost;
    };
    listen-on {
           // Ignore spoofed packets on externally
           // visible interfaces.
           127.0.0.1;     // loopback
    };
};

// Bootstrap the root.
// This is an example for overriding the defaults.
zone "." {
        type hint;
        file "named.ca";
};
```

```
// 127.0.0.0/24  The loopback network.
zone "0.0.127.in-addr.arpa" {
        type master;
        file "127.in-addr.arpa";
        allow-query {
                localhost;
        };
};
```

Complete */etc/resolv.conf* file:

```
search example.com
nameserver 127.0.0.1
```

Index

CPSIA information can be obtained at www.ICGtesting.com
Printed in the USA
LVOW082012060212

267198LV00002B/1/A

9 780979 034213